HOW TO MEND
YOUR BROKEN HEART

HOW TO MEND YOUR BROKEN HEART

Overcome Emotional Pain at the End of a Relationship

PAUL McKENNA, Ph.D.,
and
HUGH WILLBOURN, Ph.D.

 THREE RIVERS PRESS • NEW YORK

Published in the United States by Three Rivers Press,
an imprint of the Crown Publishing Group,
a division of Random House, Inc., New York.
www.crownpublishing.com

THREE RIVERS PRESS and the Tugboat design are registered
trademarks of Random House, Inc.

Originally published in Great Britain by Bantam Press,
a division of Transworld Publishers, London, in 2003.

Library of Congress Cataloging-in-Publication Data
McKenna, Paul, 1963–
    How to mend your broken heart : overcome emotional
pain at the end of a relationship / Paul McKenna and
Hugh Willbourn.— 1st American ed.
    1. Loss (Psychology) 2. Adjustment (Psychology)
3. Separation (Psychology) I. Willbourn, Hugh. II. Title.
    BF575.D35M35 2005
    155.9'3—dc22   2005002436

ISBN 1-4000-5404-4

Printed in the United States of America

DESIGN BY BARBARA STURMAN

10 9 8 7 6 5 4 3 2

First American Edition

ACKNOWLEDGMENTS

We would like to thank all our colleagues, clients, and students who have contributed to this book.

We owe a special thanks to Richard Bandler for his significant contribution to this book, including the Fall Out of Love and Threshold techniques.

For other inspiration, support, and encouragement we wish especially to thank Michael Breen, David Corr, Julie Davies, Paul Duddridge, Chrissy Iley, Michael Neill, Dariane Pictet, Jane Ralley, Clare Staples and Anne Teachworth.

Contents

How to Mend
Your Broken Heart

INTRODUCTION

This book is written for anyone who has been hurt by the end of a relationship—which is just about all of us. If you know that pain, desperation and confusion, this book is for you. Only you know the dreams you have lost and the pain it has caused. You invested a part of yourself, your future, in that relationship. When your relationship ended, that future was removed. No wonder it hurts.

At first it is difficult to believe you will ever recover. At first it is difficult to think at all because of the shock and the pain. But the drive of the life force in you keeps you going automatically. However much pain you feel, however much you cry, your heart keeps beating and your lungs keep breathing.

THE NATURAL RECOVERY MECHANISM

Every human being has within them a natural mechanism that enables them to recover from heartbreak and grief. Although millions of relationships end all over the world, people everywhere recover and go on to achieve happiness and fulfillment. Those people often say how terrible they felt months or years ago and yet now they cannot remember what they saw in their ex. Their in-built human mechanism processed the pain and made them capable of loving once again.

In some cases it takes months for that mechanism to complete its work. The proven techniques in this book make your natural healing process happen much faster and more smoothly. Using this book you can get rid of obsessional thinking, you can remove emotional pain and you can feel free to enjoy life fully again. For some people the effect is instant and dramatic; for others the effect is more gradual and they find they get better and better day by day.

It is a tough but unavoidable truth that if you loved enough to be heartbroken you simply have to experience some pain and suffering. When you lose something that mattered to you, it is natural to feel sad about it. In fact, as we shall see, it is important to feel sad about it: that feeling is an essential part of the healing process. But you do not have to experience it over and over again. You don't have to go through unnecessary suffering.

In the chapters that follow is a highly practical and purposeful approach to re-establishing emotional equilibrium in your life. The techniques described have already been used again and again to help people who have been in severe emotional pain or locked into repeating dysfunctional patterns of behavior. It is likely that you are in emotional pain right now and you want to find out how to overcome it and feel much better. If you practice the techniques outlined in this book I promise you your feelings will change radically.

Once upon a time effective pain-relief was not readily available. It was believed that pain was character-building. Nowadays, anesthetics are routinely used. They not only eliminate physical pain but, by reducing stress, they also speed up healing. Until recently, there were no straightforward techniques to deal with emotional pain, but I hope that in the same way that anesthetics have become accepted, these techniques will become widely used.

WHY THESE TECHNIQUES HELP YOU FEEL BETTER FAST

The thoughts and feelings that make up our consciousness correspond to biochemical activities in our brain. What we think affects the chemistry of our brain. Two chemicals in particular, dopamine and serotonin, play a vital part in our behavior. When we need something, dopamine is released and gives us the drive to get it. Once we've got it, we reward ourselves with a serotonin release, which makes us feel satisfied. These neurochemicals affect our feelings, just as our feelings affect the neurochemicals. If we have too much dopamine and not enough serotonin we experience a chronic feeling of craving. Some of the most painful effects of heartbreak are caused by this longing. The dopamine makes us jittery and restless, and drives us to do something, anything, to get what we want, even if we know rationally that it won't help. We get urges to go past the ex's house, call them up, talk to their friends. These urges subside when our body releases serotonin. The longing ceases and we feel calm.

The techniques in this book show you how to influence the critical variables in your thinking, which can change the neurochemicals in your mind and body. When you learn how to think about your ex in a different way you change the way your body is reacting. You no longer feel the same. You have rewritten the operating software of your brain, and you can't run the old programs anymore. The way you think about the past and the future is released from the old pattern of painful, repetitive thinking.

The ideas and the techniques build on each other and work together, so the best way to use this book is to read it all the way through first, then dip into it when you need to. Because they don't take long, you can practice a technique whenever you want. Read it through carefully a couple of times so you are quite clear about each step, then work through it methodically, putting in 100 percent of your concentration and commitment.

What you will gain from applying these techniques

Although these techniques can bring about immediate, radical change, they will not let you run away from whatever life is trying to teach you. Your pain is not meaningless. These techniques allow you to leave the pain of heartbreak behind, but life may give it back to you if you do not learn from what it is showing you. The purpose of pain is to protect you in the future.

Your pain has a specific message for you. It is about the stage of life you are at and the unconscious patterns that have been influencing your life so far. An important part of the process is bringing those patterns to conscious awareness. As you become aware of the unconscious expectations and assumptions that have been operating in your relationships, you can choose to change them if you wish.

There is an old riddle which asks, "Who learns most when a wise man meets a fool?" The answer is the wise man, because a wise man learns from everything that happens to him, and a fool never learns, even if he meets the wisest man in creation. There is wisdom to be gained from every relationship, however painful or difficult it might have been. As you use this book you can find out why things went wrong and discover how to stop it happening again. What you learn from your heartbreak makes your next relationship better.

Heartbreak is like a forest fire. For a long time it was thought that forest fires were an ecological disaster, but recently it has been learnt that fires have an essential role to play in the life of the forest. A fire burns away the undergrowth that prevented sunlight reaching the forest floor, so new plants can grow on the ashes of the old. Botanists have discovered that seeds from some redwood trees germinate only after the extreme heat of a forest fire. It turns out that even something as devastating as a forest fire contributes to the health of the forest.

A few years ago a man asked me to hypnotize him so that he would completely forget ever having met his ex-girlfriend. He wanted it to be so complete that if she came to talk to him he would think she was a stranger and say to her, "Do I know you?" That would involve eradicating the memory of his life during their relationship. Obviously I did not agree to his request. It would disrupt the continuity of his past and could make him forget essential facts about his life. But more importantly, it would treat the symptom of his distress and not the cause.

Instead I asked him what blanking her out would do for him. He replied that it would mean not thinking about her, and it would allow him to get back at her. He wanted her to feel at a loss for a change. "But if you weren't thinking about her," I asked, "would it matter to you what she felt?" He realized that leaving her behind also meant letting go of wanting to get back at her.

I told him we can't change what has happened to us but we can change how we feel about it. I helped him to reduce the pain and obsession so that he could remember everything if he wanted to but was no longer distressed by it.

Wanting to get any sort of revenge on your ex is just another way of being caught up in the relationship with them, only in a negative form. The ideal feeling to have towards your ex is not anger but neutrality. When you are truly free, you look back and feel happy about the good times and sad about the bad times, but you no longer feel wounded or attached to any of them.

THE AUTHORS

For the sake of simplicity and ease of reading we have written this book as if it were just one person speaking. Sometimes it is Paul talking, sometimes it is Hugh talking, but we have not distinguished between our contributions. We have learned from studying and teaching and between us we have worked with thousands of individuals over the years. Some of our most powerful learning has come from the wonderful people who have worked with us in therapy, in seminars and in workshops. The stories of some of those encounters are an important part of this book. Although the facts remain the same, we have changed names and identifying details in all the stories in order to protect the privacy of the individuals involved.

And we've learned a lot from our own experiences. Just like everyone else, we too have had downs as well as ups in our love life. Life continually presents each of us with fresh challenges and we learn and grow by meeting them. We don't have all the answers to all the questions raised by relationships. No one does. But what we, and our clients, have found very useful, we would like to share with you.

You are not alone

I have lost count of the number of celebrities and multi-millionaires who have told me of fears and insecurities that are just the same as everyone else's. No amount of money protects you from heartbreak. No amount of fame makes losing someone easier to bear. Sometimes people who are rich or famous feel all the more trapped because no one believes that underneath their successful exterior they are as worried as the rest of us. Everyone can have awful thoughts when a relationship ends. We can all have terrible feelings such as anger, fear, frustration, guilt, hopelessness, anxiety and despair. With this book you will be able to transform each of those feelings. But, just to start with, it's good to know you are not crazy, you are not incurable and you are not alone.

You are going through an experience that is universal and yet unique. Every human being, rich or poor, unknown or famous, has the potential to love and therefore the potential to feel heartbreak. And each of us has our own unique lesson to learn from it.

The Buddhists say that our hearts are meant to be broken because that is how they open. From that point of view it would be a great sadness to get through life without having your heart broken at least once. When relationships don't work out, we learn something about ourselves that we can't get anywhere else.

Only in relationships where we care greatly do we meet our own deepest values and the most profound imprinting that we carry from our childhood. Only when we have been opened up by love for another person do we become vulnerable and malleable enough for our experience to have such a great possibility of personal change and evolution.

1

WHAT IS HEARTBREAK?

Heartbreak is a very strange distress. It is exquisitely painful, and yet we cannot find an injury on our body. It is like one big emotional pain but it also seems to spark off hundreds of other emotions. We hate the feeling of heartbreak, and yet we find ourselves compelled to go over and over memories, ideas or fantasies which make the feeling worse. What is going on?

I can remember a relationship that ended after two years. Emotionally it fizzled out, so neither I nor my ex felt heartbroken. However, directly afterwards I had another relationship that lasted only four months but completely wrecked me because I had believed I would be with that girl forever. She used to talk about marriage, and at the time she probably meant it. I created a future in my imagination where we were a happy couple with a passionate romance and an exciting social life. I thought about what our kids might look like. All this thinking and fantasizing built up a strong network of neural pathways in my brain. As far as my nervous system was concerned, I was already married to her. When I found out she was two-timing me, in an instant my dreams and ideas seemed ridiculous. Added to all my lovely future fantasies was a huge negative feeling: Cancelled. The meaning of the pictures in my head flipped. All I could see was her in bed with another guy and think what a fool I had been. As I lay awake going over and over why this had happened, I was reinforcing how sad I felt and what a loser I must be. I felt terrible, and then even worse because I didn't know if the feeling would ever end.

One day I said to myself, "This is ridiculous! I've got to stop!" But the thoughts wouldn't stop. I didn't want to think about her, but I couldn't help it. I realized that I wasn't in charge of my own brain. I was powerless while it buzzed away. This was one of the experiences that led me eventually into writing this book. I wanted to get my mind on my side, instead of having it keep me awake at night.

When an important love relationship ends, a range of different responses is triggered. We feel loss and pain. Our normal ways of thinking about the world are disrupted. Our balance is upset, and our feelings change from one minute to the next. We pine for our ex-lover, then we are overwhelmed with anger at them. One minute we are desperate to see them, the next we can't bear to have anyone mention their name. This volatility and confusion add to the misery.

Heartbreak is caused by the end of a relationship. It can also be caused when we fail to get a relationship we fervently desire. It can even happen slowly when we realize that we are in a relationship from which all the love has gone. However it happens, after the shock, it takes some time for reality to sink in. Then we experience a welter of feelings. We can be angry, sad, devastated, despairing, distraught, desperate, remorseful, regretful, ashamed, embarrassed. The emotional bombardment is overwhelming.

In the long term, we have a natural way of dealing with these feelings. We have an emotional mechanism that allows us to recover from losses and from pain. If we didn't have it, the whole world would be in mourning forever! Bereavement, parting and suffering are unavoidable parts of our life experience. The natural way we recover is by grieving.

HOW GRIEF HEALS

Grieving is a specific process by which we gradually let go of our attachment to the people (or places or things or even possibilities) we have lost. Of course, in the first shock of heartbreak it is not much comfort to be told that things will improve in time. We might not be ready for our feelings to improve—part of us might not even have accepted what has happened yet. And even once we do accept it, it is possible to misunderstand grief. Grief happens one bit at a time. You feel bad for a while and then it stops. You feel fine, then you feel sad again, then the sadness stops. It is important to know that grief works like this, so that we are not frightened that it will carry on forever. It won't. It will stop. But while it does happen, it is important to our recovery.

You see, we experience only as much sadness as is necessary for our feelings to adjust as far as they can at any one time, then the feeling stops. When we have become used to that amount of change and loss, the unconscious lets us feel a bit more, and so on, until we have fully absorbed the whole significance of the loss. By the same token, when grief does stop, there is no need to feel guilty that we didn't care enough. Some people have told me they feel guilty about feeling all right so soon after a loss, and I have to tell them not to worry, and reassure them that they are simply being well looked after by their unconscious mind.

This process of grief can be divided into four stages. The first, denial, is where we try to reject what has happened. In the second, we accept it, but still feel angry about it. In the third stage we acknowledge our sadness, and when we reach the fourth we have accepted our loss and are able to look back and enjoy the happy memories we have.

The trouble with heartbreak, however, is that the natural process of grief does not always work properly. People can get stuck, repeating the same painful feelings over and over again. I first understood why this happened when I was working with a woman whose second husband had left her for a younger woman. Her first husband had died. As we worked together she told me, in a hesitant and ashamed tone of voice, that it had been easier to recover from being widowed than it was to recover from being left. When her first husband died her world was changed forever, but his love for her, and hers for him, was not questioned. It was an extremely painful loss, but an absolute one.

When her second husband left, it called into question the love they had had together, and the fact that he was still living in the same town made it all the more difficult for her to forget him and move on. It is these sorts of questions about the past and the future that can make heartbreak so painful and complicated.

None of us can avoid feeling some pain and sadness at the end of a relationship we cared about—as we will see, a certain amount is even necessary. But this book is dedicated to helping you avoid the unnecessary repetition of pain and distress. It helps you change the way you think and feel about the past and the future by working with your fundamental systems of thought and feeling. Better still, as you make these changes and understand them, you prepare yourself for a richer and stronger relationship in the future.

THE THREE CORE SYSTEMS
OF HUMAN BEING

I remember attending a conference of psychotherapists and hypnotherapists nearly fifteen years ago and being struck by something most peculiar. There were lots and lots of different speakers and nearly all of them were clearly caring, intelligent and competent therapists. However, it became apparent that each of them understood human beings differently. That seemed to me a bit odd. After all, psychotherapists spend all their working lives dealing with human beings, so you might expect them to know and agree about what human beings are. But it was clear that there was no single, agreed understanding of what a human being is.

That conference inspired me to do a considerable amount of research in psychotherapy and philosophy to discover if there was a central understanding of what a human being is, about which we could all agree. While I was doing that, a number of American researchers were making very important breakthroughs in understanding the connection between the mind and the body. Bringing together all this research added up to a rich and complex set of insights into the human being. And, as well as the philosophical and psycho-biological findings, it also let us produce a practical method to heal a broken heart.

The essential insight is this. Human beings are in essence a combination of three things:

- The conscious mind;
- The unconscious mind;
- The physiological system of the body.

These three systems coexist and interrelate. Our intelligence and our emotions function in each of these three systems. All our magnificent potential as human beings lies in these systems, and an understanding of this simple model of the human being is all that is needed to begin to learn how to make lasting personal change.

You could also say that these three systems are simply different aspects of the same thing, or three parts of one system. And it is equally true that there are other important and subtle processes in our being that we are not discussing here. But we will talk about these three systems here because it is the easiest and most useful way to understand what is going on in heartbreak, and how to recover and move on.

The conscious mind

We do our active thinking in our conscious mind. The conscious mind is our immediate awareness of what is around us, and the thoughts and pictures we use in our head. It is the voice with which we talk to ourselves, the ideas we are paying attention to, and our ability to make decisions.

It is the part of ourselves with which we are most familiar, and yet in a way it is our most mysterious part. Scientists have tried for decades to understand how it works and to locate it exactly in the body. Philosophers have tried for centuries to define consciousness. Technologists have struggled in vain to replicate consciousness with artificial intelligence computers. A lot of questions remain to be answered, but we can now make a clear definition of the conscious mind.

The conscious mind is two interdependent processes: awareness, and the creation of meaning. The first is fairly obvious. Consciousness is always awareness of something—we use the word "conscious" as a synonym for awake or aware. The second process is not so obvious, partly because making sense of things is an aspect of our awareness. For example, as I type this sentence, I can see a vase of flowers on the table next to me. I don't usually pay attention to the fact, but it is I who gives meaning to my sensory impressions and hence sees them as flowers.

A more dramatic demonstration of this would be what happens when I interrupt that process. One of my favorite routines in my stage show is to hypnotize a man to fail to recognize his own girlfriend (or the other way around). With hypnosis I am switching off that part of the meaning-making process that recognizes people. My hypnotic subject still sees a woman, but he does not recognize her because we understand what we see only when we bring meaning to it. All perception, whether real or imaginary, is made up in part of the meaning we give it.

The unconscious mind

The unconscious mind stores and runs the programs of automatic behavior that we use to live our lives. You could say that it is the part of our memory, thinking and mental activity of which we are unaware at any one time.

Human beings have evolved the ability to carry out

tasks without using deliberate intention. We could spend hours considering all the different alternatives open to us every day, but we don't have the time for it. In order not to waste our days considering millions of choices, we've developed a capacity for automatic responses.

For example, we tend to have the same sort of breakfast every morning. We don't ask ourselves, Shall I have a boiled egg? Shall I have some cereal? We only ask these questions on special occasions or holidays. On ordinary days we have the same thing we normally have. We usually take the same route to work, read the same newspaper and listen to the same radio station. We have habits of cooking and eating. We have habits to tie our shoelaces and comb our hair. We do a thousand and one daily tasks without having to think about them, simply by using habits. Habits keep our lives running smoothly.

The unconscious mind is where we store and run the habits we have created. It is our autopilot. You don't have to think about the knot in order to tie your shoelaces; you do it on autopilot. When you were a small child you had to concentrate fiercely to tie your laces properly but now you literally don't think about it. You brush your teeth on autopilot. You can even drive to work, perfectly safely, while thinking about your plans for the day ahead. Your autopilot watches the road while you are thinking about something else. As soon as the autopilot spots something potentially hazardous or unusual, it calls your full attention back to the road.

The basic mechanism of these habits is association.

Our unconscious mind remembers when we do two things together, and if we keep doing them together, pretty soon the first one triggers the second. In the morning the alarm rings and we get up and go to the bathroom. We go into the kitchen and switch on the kettle. Soon we make bigger habits out of lots of little ones all joined together.

These habits are useful because they free our conscious minds to think about other things. But as we shall see, sometimes we need to change or override them. Many of us as children were ordered to eat every bit of food on our plate, for example. Many adults continue to let this habit run their behavior. They carry on eating even when they are no longer hungry and they end up eating more, and weighing more, than they want to.

When you are heartbroken, lots of unhelpful habits in your life need changing, and we are going to show you how to do this.

Physiology

The third system of human being is physiology: the body. The body is an obvious part of our being but some of its most amazing features are hidden from us. It is not just a machine that does what it is told. It has its own intelligence: the autonomic nervous system. This is the system that regulates your heartbeat and your breathing, making sure your muscles get the oxygen you need. It also regulates the digestive system and your cycle of sleep and wakefulness. It has its own method of self-preservation, the fight or flight response, which can be triggered without any intervention from the conscious mind. When you hear a loud noise and find yourself tense and alert, your body has triggered the fight or flight response before you have had time to think about it. You are ready to run away immediately or fight for your life.

All our mental and emotional activity has a corresponding component in our body. The way our thoughts and feelings are connected to the body has only recently been thoroughly investigated by scientists. Our thoughts and actions correspond to patterns of activity in the brain called neural pathways. When we repeat the same thought or action, we strengthen the associated neural pathway. In other words, events in the conscious and unconscious mind influence events in the body.

The effect works in the other direction too. The state of our body has a direct effect on the state of our conscious and unconscious minds. If we have physical tension in the body it corresponds to emotional tension in the mind. Since what we do with our body affects what goes on in our mind, this means that by making physical changes we can alter how we feel.

INTERCONNECTION

The three systems are three distinct aspects of each human being. We exist and operate simultaneously in all of them. No one system can exist without the others.

What is more, our own experience cannot be reduced to, or fully described at, just one level. It would be absurd to say that we are just chemical machines, or that we are only what we think, or that we are just a collection of unconscious programs. The whole of a human being is greater than the sum of these parts.

However, the crucial point is that each aspect influences the others. If we make changes at any one of these three levels, we change the whole person. In this book we will be working on all three systems, sometimes individually, sometimes all at once.

Emotions operate in and affect all three systems. The story we tell ourselves in our conscious minds influences the emotional meaning we give to the events we perceive. Equally, the memory of events in the past, and the anticipation of events in the future, can occur at an unconscious level, giving rise to quite separate emotional responses. Thirdly, the state of our bodies evokes other emotional responses. For example, people who are depressed tend to move slowly, to sit or lie down for long periods and to stare and frown a lot. If you put your body into that posture, sooner or later you begin to feel like that. Happy people typically look ahead, upwards and around them. They smile and laugh frequently. Their bodies are relaxed and not hunched up. If you put your body in an upright, relaxed posture and let a smile play on your face you will soon begin to feel uplifted.

Heartbreak affects all three systems

If you had thought, "Easy come, easy go," about your relationship you wouldn't be heartbroken. By definition, heartbreak is what you feel when you didn't want the relationship to end. There can be all sorts of complications, of course. Some of us find partners so difficult and exasperating that we can hardly live with them—but we are fairly sure we can't live without them, either. Some of us only realize after we have split up how deep the attachment was to our partner. Whatever the situation, sooner or later the reality hits home. Your partner is gone, and you miss them. And that is, as the saying goes, a shock to the system. And as we shall see, that phrase is remarkably accurate.

Heartbreak is a shock that impacts on all three systems of our being. The emotional shock to your consciousness when you realize a relationship is over is so severe that it causes a physical reaction. At a physiological level the body does not distinguish between an emotional threat and a physical threat. First it goes into shock, then, because it cannot find a physical solution to the emotional pain, the shock leads to stress. The body has prepared itself by triggering the fight or flight response. Blood flow is directed away from the body's surface to the major muscles, adrenaline is released and digestion is halted. But there is no one to fight and nowhere to run. So the body does not get any clear signals to release this state of tension and heightened alertness. Getting stuck like this is called "stress," and if it happens for long periods it is bad for your health.

RELEASING STRESS

Luckily, as we saw above, just as the mind can influence the body, so can the body influence the mind. When you find a way to let the body release the tension it feels calmer and more comfortable, and that in turn affects your mood. Your emotions calm down, and you can concentrate better or relax and sleep soundly.

The simplest way to help the body relax is to use up the energy and alertness for action it has prepared—in other words, to get some exercise. It doesn't have to be anything grand. If you are not used to exercise, just a brisk walk is helpful. If you are a bit fitter, you may need to work out a bit more. The point is simply to use up the tension and energy and trigger the body's natural relaxation, which is called the parasympathetic response. It is the sweet, soft feeling you get in your muscles when your body relaxes after hard work or vigorous movement. You also feel a high caused by the release of endorphins, the body's natural opiates. This relaxation is as nice as stress is nasty. You can give yourself an easy, positive boost simply by getting ten to fifteen minutes of brisk exercise in the day.

The two points to remember here are these:

• This is not a fitness regime or self-punishment. If you want to use the chance to get fitter, that's fine, but all you actually need to do is just enough exercise to use up excess tension. A brisk fifteen-minute walk will do that.

• Don't be put off just because you don't feel like going for a walk or taking some exercise today. You are doing this to get your emotional state comfortable and balanced—the fact that you don't feel like it is more than likely a symptom of feeling low, which is exactly what sensible exercise will help to relieve.

Several clinical trials have found that the single most effective therapy for depression—whatever its initial cause—was simply asking patients to get a reasonable amount of physical exercise each day.

Heartbreak in the conscious mind

One of the most relentless causes of pain in splitting up is the constant circulation of thoughts in the conscious mind. But precisely how does a thought hurt? It might seem a bit odd to ask the question. After all, it's obvious. It just feels awful. But when you look a bit closer, it becomes mysterious. For example, if you stub your toe, you can describe the type of pain as "aching" or "throbbing." As for where it is, "It's in my toe." But where is the pain of heartbreak? And what exactly is it? And why is it that whatever your friends say, and however much they care, it doesn't seem to make the feeling any better? There is certainly tension in the solar plexus, beneath the navel, but is that heartbreak? No, it is more than that. There is sadness when you think about being on your own, but that is not the whole of it. Why is it so painful? Why is it so difficult to pin down? Why is it so difficult to get over? Why does it feel so desperate?

The answer to all these questions lies in the nature of the conscious mind. As we saw earlier, the conscious mind receives our perceptions and attaches meaning to them. Meanings make things matter to us. Everything in our conscious mind, what we see around us and the thoughts and pictures we make in our heads, all have meaning. And the fundamental kind of human meaning is narrative, or stories. A story is an event going from the past to the future. Whether it is true or fictional, the essence of a story is that something has already happened and something else is going to happen next—in the future. Our minds make sense of our lives by relating the present to the past and the future. That is, by creating narratives.

When your heart is broken, all that meaning is thrown up in the air. Your future is taken to pieces and your past is called into question. How can you have reached this point of heartbreak when you thought you loved each other? How was your love betrayed?

BETRAYAL

Every heartbreak is in some way a betrayal. It is a betrayal of the promise of love. It was a promise made in the past that was a commitment to the future. For some of us that promise was still a secret, or a dream. No vows were taken, no commitment was formally made, but in our heart we were hoping that this relationship would last. With our heart we were already committed; we were just waiting for our partner to catch up. But, sadly, it turned out that the partner had a different idea. This relationship was not to be their destination. They were just passing through.

For others the end of a relationship is the betrayal of a promise made at the altar. Someone couldn't live up to the commitment they made. Sometimes people are betrayed by their lover or a friend; other times we betray ourselves. We have affairs. We start things that spiral out of control. It is all too easy to underestimate the forces of attraction, be it lust or love, until it is too late. And it is too easy to take what we have for granted, or to let ourselves be taken for granted, and then to lose what we have treasured.

THE MEANING OF HEARTBREAK

Every moment of the day we are making sense of our lives in terms of the future—even in the simplest things. The primary way in which we understand the things around us is by using them. We don't see a flat, rigid, rectangular horizontal surface supported at each corner by a vertical stick and deduce that it is a table and theorize about its function. We just use it. It is a table: something for putting things on. We understand things in terms of what they are for and what we can use them to do. In other words, we understand things in terms of their possibilities. And possibilities exist in the future. To say something is possible is to say that some time in the future it could happen.

We also use the past in making sense of things. You make sense of this sentence as you read it by remembering the beginning while reaching forward to the end. The meaning we make of life depends on our experiences in the past and our expectations of the future.

When you are in a relationship, your partner is an important part of your future. When we describe caring a great deal for someone, we often say, "They mean so much to me." Anyone we care for a great deal means a lot to us. And if they mean a lot to us, they are involved in our future.

When you are heartbroken, the future you dreamed of is demolished and the past is undermined. No wonder heartbreak is so painful and so confusing. It feels like nothing in the here and now can make a difference, because it is the past and the future that hurt. The meaning you had built has been cancelled. Healing a broken heart means building a new future and creating a new relationship with your past.

FEAR OF THE UNKNOWN

With a broken heart, instead of heading towards a future we had planned and were looking forward to, we face the unknown. This is what many people fear most—not death, not illness, but the unknown. Not only have we lost the relationship we wanted, we have ended up with something we didn't want, and most of us actually fear. And we feel desperate, because the conscious mind is trying to make a meaning, any meaning, of an unknown future.

Much of the activity of technologically advanced societies is devoted to controlling and avoiding the unknown. Hence we are not used to facing it. The less experience we have of it, the more we fear it. However, in societies in which materialism is less entrenched, the unknown is traditionally welcomed, because it leads to new discoveries and deeper understanding. The truth is that if we learn something radically new it will disrupt our previous beliefs and understanding. Anything genuinely new and different cannot be derived from what we already know. Real progress comes from letting go of old beliefs and letting new ones emerge. The process of letting go is stepping into the unknown.

Of course, when you got heartbroken you were not setting out to learn anything new or to change your future. In fact, you would rather it hadn't happened at all. However, the fact of the matter is that it did happen, and it has changed your future and you don't yet know how or when you are going to feel better. The point is that right now, for a little while, it is well worth getting used to the unknown. It is a stepping stone on the way to healing your heart.

MODES OF THINKING

Faced with the unknown, the mind automatically looks for ways to plan the future and explain the past. It tries to reduce the anxiety by creating all manner of thoughts by which to understand and deal with what's going on. These thoughts are words and pictures in our head. **The pictures in our head and the things we say to ourselves profoundly affect how we feel.** The pictures we make and the things we say when we are heartbroken are mostly very uncomfortable.

Maybe you thought about your partner and said to yourself, "He's not coming back." Maybe you recalled some of the good times and said to yourself, "It will never be the same again." You might have asked yourself, "What did I do wrong?" and then conjured up all kinds of things and started saying, "It's all my fault because . . ." Or you might have thought about your ex being somewhere else, with someone else, and you being stuck here on your own. All these thoughts, and hundreds of others like them, contribute to feeling bad after a breakup.

We all know this, of course. We know how bad this kind of thinking makes us feel, but somehow it seems terribly difficult to stop. More and more, the mind is filled with painful, uncomfortable and unhelpful images. These thoughts go round and round and escalate and increase because our mind is trying to figure out a way of rescuing the situation. Unfortunately, it is making things worse. Repeatedly seeing the pictures and thinking the thoughts is building up a habit of feeling bad. It is reinforcing the neural pathways that correspond to lack of self-worth, sadness and heartbreak, which before long will begin to run on automatic. Soon, anything even remotely related to your ex—a place you once went to together, the mention of their name, a film you both saw, a mutual friend, the drink they liked, even someone with the same color hair—will fire off a neuroelectric charge down the pathways of heartbreaking feelings you have established. The feeling of heartbreak has been programmed into you. Instantly, you can be reduced to utter sadness. This is no longer love. It is no longer the genuine sorrow of parting. It is simply repetitive and unnecessary pain. In the next chapter I will show you how to change the patterns of your thinking so that you can escape from this trap, and free yourself from all that unnecessary pain.

2

How do I stop feeling so bad?

When you get out of a relationship, you find yourself on your own, rattling round with a set of habits built for two. Much of the pain of heartbreak comes from expectations and habits that are running all by themselves but are no longer appropriate. You are used to coming home to someone in the evening, to having someone to discuss things with, to having someone to go out with. And whether you stay in or go out, you keep finding reminders of your ex all over your life. The cafés you used to visit, the games you used to play, all the things you used to do have now got associations with your ex.

A lot of these associations are obvious. You have probably already found yourself avoiding some of the places you used to go to because it can be upsetting. However, some associations are fainter, more subliminal. They can affect you even though they may not be powerful enough to reach the level of conscious awareness. Without being aware of it you might associate your ex with certain rooms, even with the chair they used to sit in or the programs they used to watch. These associations set off trains of thought that cause you to dwell on the past far more than you want to, and more than you need to. I am now going to show you exactly how to get rid of the habits that are holding you back. You will learn how to modify the way you look at the past and the future so that you can free yourself from the pain, and the mistakes, of the past. Whether those mistakes were yours or your ex-partner's doesn't matter. It doesn't matter now who, if anyone, was to blame. What matters is how to move on.

Tell me the truth about love

Quite often, when I tell my clients they really can leave that old relationship behind, something strange happens. It is as though there has been a change of atmosphere in the room. Some people cross their arms or pull their clothes around them as if they were cold. Some change the subject; others sit back in their chair and look at me as though they have decided that I am not to be trusted. They might even smile at me, while all the rest of their body language is saying, "No."

This change of attitude happens because they have realized that I am serious, that there is a real chance right now to begin full and complete separation from that past relationship. As this reality sinks in, a bit of them says something like this: "No. Even though it hurts, even though I feel a pain I can hardly bear, even though my life is a mess, even though I can't see any way of making the relationship work, even though my head tells me it will bring me nothing but trouble, I don't want to let go!" Or this: "In spite of everything, I still love my ex, whatever they did to me. In spite of the pain, the exhaustion, the hopelessness, if I believe in love, I've got to hang on."

When I hear variations of this, and I see and feel the sincerity and the desperation of the person who is talking to me, I remember all the lies that are told about love.

The poet W. H. Auden pleaded, "Oh tell me the truth about love," but never got a definitive answer. At one level love is a neurochemical event, but at other levels it is a great mixture of feelings and wishes and actions and changes. We find it in great moments of passion and heroism, and we find it in a cup of coffee or the touch of a fingertip. Love is all of these, and always more than we could ever say about it. When love is smiling on us, we get on fine without defining it. When we are crossed in love, we try night and day to discover its secrets. What does love ask, how does it work, what does it mean, what can we do, what can we hope for? When love has been and gone, and one person still loves and the other has moved on, one of us is left with heart-break. It is clear that love, whatever it is, does not totally transform everything about us. It adds up to something magical, but it doesn't remove the fact that we are ordinary human beings with ordinary human failings. All of us can be selfish or annoying, harsh or demanding, needy or bossy, kind or cruel, caring or thoughtless. When love has fled, it leaves exposed the less than wonderful parts of exes and ourselves.

One of the most painful parts of heartbreak is the feeling of need for that person; the feeling of helplessness, abandonment, incompleteness, even desperation. It feels as though there is an immense void in your life which only one person can fill, and that person has gone. This horrible feeling, which we call neediness, is actually a combination of two things: a fear and an attachment.

The fear is of aloneness, of being on your own and being solely responsible for yourself and your feelings. In a relationship we learn to look after each other's feelings one way or another. We can even become dependent on someone we argue with or have to look after all the time. We can get so used to doing things with some-one else that we forget how to look after ourselves on our own. For some of us, remembering, or even discovering, how to do that is scary, so we don't even want to look in that direction. Instead, we stare stubbornly at the departing figure of our ex and shout, "I want you to do it for me!"

The other part of neediness is attachment. The attachment is the identification with your ex. It is the sense that they are part of your existence. A part of you does not want to see your ex as a separate person who is going their own way. That person was part of your world, part of your future, part of your understanding of life, part of you. So when you broke up, a part of you did leave, and that hurts. Because accepting this feeling seems so hard at first, we tend to treat it as a problem that would be solved if only someone else behaved differently, rather than an event that requires us to accept a change in ourselves. It is simpler to say, "I need him," or "I need her," than it is to say, "I need to change how I understand myself." However much we love or loved the other person, in the end each of us is in charge of our own feelings. If that wasn't true, the ex could just press a button, make you feel better and then leave again.

Another version of this issue, which also comes up when people face the reality of leaving a past relationship behind forever, is the belief that the ex was "the only one for me." This statement is both true and false. Simply put, there was a time when your partner was the only one for you, but as time passes the truth changes and now this belief is false. It doesn't make it any less true in the past. A relationship between people is not an object but an event that is continually happening. "You are the only one for me" is true only as long as both people are making it true.

That might sound complicated, but it isn't. Think for a moment of a type of food you loved as a child but don't really care for now. When you were younger, it was true that you liked it, and now it is true that you don't. What has changed is your taste, your relationship to that food. When I was young I loved jelly. I could have eaten it every day. But now I can take it or leave it. Mostly, I leave it. When people stay happily in a faithful relationship, one of the things they are doing is maintaining the truth of the statement "You are the one for me." If they stop doing it, the relationship begins to change and break down, and eventually the statement is no longer true.

Love is not neediness. Love is not fear and attachment. Love is not attachment at all. But because we are not perfect and we are not saints, all of us have a certain amount of attachment mixed up with our love, and all of us are happy to have some shelter at times from the loneliness of being.

Deep down all of us know that love means wishing the very best for the loved one. As that loved one is a human being with free will, it also means respecting their wish to be separate from you. It means wishing them well on their path through life. If that path leads away from you, love does not hold them back. It wishes them well as they tread that path. You might think it would be nice if they returned, but love is total acceptance of their freedom to leave you forever. Love values their freedom, their personal evolution and their happiness above the pleasure you receive from being with them. Love also knows that two lovers can only fully enjoy love that is freely given. Love knows that if you attempt to hold on to your lover against their will, eventually their love will wither and die and your own will decay into jealousy.

Love is the wish for the good of the other person. When we use the word "love" to describe our longing for that other person we may be talking about "in-love-ness" or passion or whatever, but that is not pure love.

Of course, it is rare to find a relationship that does not have some neediness. Neediness is a typical failing about which loving partners are understanding and good-humored, but it is never the basis of a healthy relationship. If your partner chose to leave you, love says you must let them go. Every mother is sad to see her children grow up and leave home—but she lets them go because she loves them. She knows that if she keeps them at home she will stifle their chance to grow, to make their own decisions and their own way in life, and eventually to have children of their own.

If you have loved someone who has left you, you have played an important part in their life. The pair of you have shared special times. You can enjoy the memory of those times if you truly let the person go in your heart. Imagine giving them a new and different future as you look forward to a new and different future for yourself. If you stay attached to a notion of a future with your ex, those memories will be painful. If you release that old view of the future and turn towards a new one, these memories will eventually be a source of joy. The techniques in this book help you to do that.

MOVING ON

For most of us, it still feels hard to let go of a secret desire that somehow a miracle will make everything all right again. So it's time to take the first steps towards your new future. The steps are easy, and will help you to feel better straight away without having to think about your ex at all.

This is a time of change. Some of the changes you make will become your new habits, so it is a good idea to choose now the sort of habits you want to live with in your future. Do you want to change your diet? Is there something you've been meaning to start but never seemed to have time? Now is your opportunity to start a new regime, take up a new sport or explore a change of lifestyle.

As we have already seen, even the everyday details of your life could have subliminal associations with your ex which cause you unnecessary suffering. It makes a lot of sense to change some of those details, by however little. If you have moved house because of the end of your relationship then you may have lost your home but you do have an opportunity to start afresh with completely new associations.

If you are still living in the same place, take a good look around your environment. What changes have you been wanting to make that you haven't got round to doing? Were you going to buy something new for your home? Does the kitchen need a touch of paint? How about rearranging the furniture? If you have a set place where you talk on the telephone, why not change it? Each piece of furniture in your home is positioned in a matrix that is associated with your old life. As you move the furniture, even if only a little, you disrupt the conscious and unconscious associations that it held for you.

So put the table at a different angle, move the telephone to the other side of the bed, swap things around in the living room. This may seem trivial, but it is very powerful, and just how powerful it can be is easy to prove. Do it. Do it today. Do it now. If you are at home, get up right now and move the chair, sofa, bed or whatever you were sitting on so that you see your own home, your own familiar room, from a different angle.

Right, you've done that, now plan to do some more. Find a new way to arrange the stuff in your home so that it is ready to collect some new, healthy, liberated associations. How about changing the colors? Or consider getting something new to change the feeling of a room. You don't have to spend a lot of money. Just get a new cushion or two, a drape, a throw or a new picture.

The point of these changes is to break up the old associations and give yourself a new environment for your new life. The changes you make don't have to be permanent or perfect. Just try something out for a few days, and keep experimenting or changing until you find a new color scheme, arrangement or layout that suits you. Don't feel obliged to stick with your first attempt—but *do* change something, even if it is just using a different shampoo and deleting your ex's number from the memory of your cell phone. Change something. ***Now.***

GETTING THE HABITS OF YOUR
MIND ON YOUR SIDE

By changing the layout and colors of your environment you have broken the old pattern of external associations. The next step is to do the same thing on the inside. Some of the commonest causes of pain in heartbreak are unintentional—literally. They are the automatic habits of thought, the pictures we make and the things we say to ourselves every day.

These habits are the "furniture" in our mind. We've got used to having them there and we use them every day. They are so familiar we don't have to think about them. Many of these habits are run completely automatically by the unconscious mind.

Some of the deepest habits are ones we created without even realizing it when we were little children. As we shall see, some of them might not be very helpful. In fact, most of us go through life with unnecessary habits that we picked up by accident and use simply because we didn't realize we could change them.

In a relationship, we build up a huge array of habits of thought and behavior. When we have intense experiences we can create habits, particularly habits of thought, extremely quickly, so even a brief or difficult relationship can create a multitude of internal habits. When the relationship ends, these patterns can still be running, even though they are no longer appropriate. Worse than that, they make it painful. We don't mean to do it. We make ourselves unhappy by accident.

Other habits are created by the intense experience of splitting up, such as the habit of thinking about the ex-partner and repeating the fact that they have gone. **Negative feelings are maintained by the repetition of the thoughts and pictures that trigger unhappy feelings. When we stop repeating them, the feelings decay.**

One of the most powerful ways to start mending your broken heart is to change the habits of your thinking. It is easy to do, it makes you feel better straight away, and it cuts out a vast amount of emotional pain that you didn't need to feel anyway.

THE POWER OF PERSPECTIVE

In order to change your thinking habits easily and successfully you need to understand a little more about how you create your perception and feelings from moment to moment. Have you ever witnessed the same event as someone else and found out later that their account of it was completely different to yours? You were in the same place at the same time but you each perceived what happened very differently. The difference arises in part from the neurophysiological state each of you was in. Your emotional state and your specific interests made you filter the available information differently from the other person. This is why, although we all live in the same world, we have so many disagreements about how we should look after it. The facts may be the same, but you bring your own meanings to them. If you accumulate experiences of feeling negative about your life, you teach yourself to see life negatively. If you accumulate positive states, you teach yourself to see life positively.

The way you make sense of the world, the meaning you bring to what you see, is a function of the point of view, or frame, through which you see things. This frame is made of your internal habits, beliefs and feelings, and the external data you include. There is no absolutely fixed meaning to anything in life. Everything is affected by the point of view you bring to it, and the meaning of anything depends on what you include or exclude from your frame of perception.

One reason why some people handle the end of a relationship better than others is because of the way they interpret the event, the frame they see it through. Over the years I have had the opportunity to work with people who have undergone terrible tragedies but whose perspectives gave them an amazing strength that enabled them to handle the pain. Equally I have seen people devastated by a relatively small challenge. It's down to the framing the individual uses.

A photographer uses framing to tell you what is important in a picture. He or she chooses the proportions, the point of view and the angle so that your eye is drawn to the elements the photographer wants you to notice. The frames we use when we see things, think about things and make pictures in our mind have a huge influence on the way we interpret our experiences. A painful memory, for example, can be overwhelming when thought of in the time frame of a few minutes surrounding the event. However, its importance may well change when thought of in the context of a lifetime.

Many modern therapists now use the art of "reframing" to help people reinterpret problems and find new solutions. The ability to reframe gives us more choices; it makes us more powerful. However, in order to do it, we need to develop a greater flexibility in our thinking. I have found that people who get over difficulties well rarely see what happens to them as a disaster or tragedy—they frame it as a challenge instead. What someone else might consider a terrible event, they see as an opportunity. We can all do this. We just have to look at a situation in a certain way, put the incident in a positive context. It is not a matter of "true" or "false"; it is a matter of a point of view. It is not what happens to us, it is how we interpret it, that determines the outcome.

As you become better at the art of reframing, you give yourself more choices in life. The more choices you have, the more flexible you are. And the more flexible you are, the wider your range of potential responses. Being heartbroken can feel like having nothing worth doing and no means of changing anything, but that is because the frame you are using is too narrow and limiting. Learning to see yourself and your situation with a different frame is a wonderful liberation. And anything can be reframed.

For example, think back to a mistake you once made. Now ask yourself what you could teach someone by telling them the story of that mistake. Whatever you teach them, you have transformed your "mistake" into a teaching aid. What's more, you too can learn what you taught them! One of my favorite reframes is a saying of Tom Watson, the man who started IBM. He said that if you want to double your success rate you first have to be prepared to double your failure rate. In that context, the risk of failure is seen as a reasonable risk on the path to success.

Another useful reframe is a question I use to understand somebody who is doing something I find spiteful, wrong or unpleasant. I ask myself: What is the positive intention behind this behavior? On the whole, most people do have good intentions. When they are scared or angry they express them defensively but it is very useful indeed to use the frame of positive intention to understand more about an action that seems to you to be wrong.

When the great Indian hero Mahatma Gandhi was negotiating with the British administration to win freedom for the Indian nation he thought long and hard about the motivation behind British behavior. He could see how the British were trying to protect their empire but he also imagined that they were trying to look after the interests of the Indian people as well. Although Gandhi thought British methods were oppressive he could view the British administrators as trying to do what they thought was best. Whether he was "right" or "wrong" didn't matter. Gandhi's attitude allowed him to approach the negotiations from a resourceful perspective that was ultimately successful.

REFRAMING PERSPECTIVES

Here's an excellent exercise that will help you to look at your circumstances from different points of view so that you gain helpful insights. You might get a sudden breakthrough straightaway, or maybe lots of flashes in the next day or so.

1. Think about the breakup of your relationship. What are the judgments or generalizations you have made about yourself and your ex?

2. Now think of someone you admire. It can be a friend, a mentor or a character from history. Imagine he or she is watching a movie of this part of your life, and step into their shoes to watch it instead. Imagine what their comments would be.

3. Now imagine a completely neutral observer is watching the movie of your life. Step into their shoes and watch it from there. What do you notice about the interaction from this neutral perspective?

4. Notice the differences, however small or large, you see from each point of view. Which ones are helpful? Which ones make you feel better? Use these perspectives to see your relationship differently.

THE POWER OF INTERNAL STATES

A state can be defined as "the sum total of all the neurobiological processes occurring within somebody at any one time." A more simple way of describing a state is "the mood you are in." The frame you are using affects the state you are in, and the state you are in influences the frame you are using. Quite simply, happiness, anger, confidence, fear, apathy, fascination and so on are states and they affect the way we see the world around us. We are constantly moving into different states of being all day long and each of them is individual and unique to us. Something happens to us and we react to it by changing state automatically. You see someone you are attracted to and that changes your state. You have to give a presentation to a group of people and that changes your state.

With the pictures we make in our imagination and the way we talk to ourselves, we create our own personal map of the world. This is our internal representation, and it determines how we understand reality. If we draw our map of the world based on beliefs that life is boring and unpleasant, then our life will reflect that. If the beliefs we use to draw our map of the world are filled with happiness and excitement, our life will reflect this. That is why we always get more of what we focus on in life.

Of course, being in love, or "in-love-ness," is a state. Whatever else they are, and however we feel or understand them, all feelings, including love, are physiological, neurochemical events. This means that when we say or do certain things, especially with someone to whom we are close, our brains fire off chemical and electrical impulses which create those well-known feelings in us. However, for this state to be maintained, to feel like we are in love with someone, we have to build a habit of focusing upon all the things we like about them.

Freud compared being in love to being hypnotized. Hypnosis allows us to focus on some things and not others so that we can relax deeply, forget to smoke, or dance like a ballerina in front of a laughing audience without embarrassment. When we are in love we focus tightly on what is adorable about the one we love, and let that feeling influence all our perceptions.

So how does this apply to the way you feel about your former partner? A major source of unnecessary distress in heartbreak is thinking about your ex with your "in-love" map still in place. This distress can be reduced, and for some people eliminated, by changing how you represent your ex in your mind, by redrawing your map. Whenever we think of someone, we create an internal representation of them. We visualize them. Most of the time, we do this quite automatically and the image is just another part of the landscape of our mental activity. Whether we are aware of it or not, we are using visualizations all the time. It's probably only when you are asked to do this deliberately that you become aware of how you think of someone, how you "see" them in your mind's eye.

USING VISUALIZATION

Everybody has the ability to visualize. If you are not sure how you visualize, then answer this simple question: Which side of your front door is the lock on? Take enough time to be sure of the answer. In order to answer that question you have to use your imagination and make a picture of your front door. Making a picture like this is called "visualization." It is a specific cognitive activity, and recently scientists have been able to pinpoint the part of our brain that we use to make these internal pictures.

Some people are more adept than others at visualization and seem to make richer pictures, but their skill is just a matter of degree, not difference. They are more aware of their capacity to visualize but they are not physiologically different from the rest of us. Artists, photographers and designers all have a highly developed capacity for visualization precisely because they have to use it so much. However, every single one of us makes pictures in our imagination, and we can all learn how to change the pictures we are making.

When you picture something in your imagination, it may not be as vivid as in real life; there might be less color, or the image is transparent. Interestingly, the imaginary space in which we see things seems to have a direction relative to each individual. We see things to the left or the right, slightly above or slightly below our sight line, in front of us or off to the side, or towards the edge of the visual field. This space of imaginary visualization coexists with our ordinary perception; it doesn't replace ordinary perception but happens alongside it.

There is a very simple way to demonstrate your visualization skills. Remember your front door again now, and notice what color it is. Now imagine what it would look like if it was bright orange or had yellow stripes down it. Make it bigger. Now move it away so that it is smaller. Move it further away and down a bit so you are looking down on it. You can play with it in all sorts of different ways and see it from different angles, at different distances and so on.

In ancient Greece and Rome orators would remember their lengthy speeches by calling to mind their own homes and visualizing symbols to represent each point they were going to make. They would see the first symbol outside the front door, the second one inside, the third one in the next room, and so on. That's where the phrase "In the first place . . ." comes from, which people use when assembling arguments. In the last few decades psychologists have rediscovered the power and significance of visualization and have developed the extremely powerful techniques that we can use today. We will be using some of these new ways to change the pictures in your mind very soon.

So why is visualization important? It is important because our feelings respond to the pictures we make in our mind. It is part of the meaning-making process. **When we think of a person, how we feel about them is coded in how we represent them in our mind.**

Our body reacts to what we imagine vividly in the

same way that it reacts to what we really encounter. We react to what our attention focuses on, whether it is real or imaginary, actually happening or remembered. Memory and imagination affect our feelings in the same way as reality does. **We are constantly affecting our state by the pictures we make in our imagination and the way we talk to ourselves.**

CHANGING THE VARIABLES

Our feelings are very closely linked to the precise way in which we remember or imagine things. **Changing the variables in a visualization changes the feelings it evokes.** You will notice that some changes have a bigger effect than others. Generally speaking, images that are closer, bigger, brighter and more colorful have greater emotional intensity than those that are duller, smaller and further away.

One of the most significant variables is whether you are inside the memory seeing what you saw and hearing what you heard at the time, or whether you are standing outside the memory watching yourself and the situation you were in as if it were a movie. Seeing a memory from the inside is called "associated memory." Seeing it from the outside is called "dissociated memory." Soon I will show you a technique that will demonstrate how to move from one to the other, and how powerful it is to do so.

Conditioning

The brain is a mass of millions of neural pathways with each idea or memory moving along its own route. Whenever we have an intense experience, our brain encodes into our nervous system a memory of the sequence of behavior that led to it. Whenever we do something new we create a neural pathway so we can access that experience again easily. Each time we repeat that behavior we strengthen the neural pathway; indeed, the neural pathway actually gets physically bigger through repetition.

In the 1900s a Russian scientist called Pavlov conducted some pioneering psychological experiments. The most famous of these was an experiment in which he rang a bell whenever he fed his dogs. After he had done this several times the dogs associated the bell with food and within a short while he would only have to ring the bell for the dogs to start salivating. There was no link between bells and food until Pavlov created one. This process, known as "conditioned response," is exactly the same one by which people become hardwired to certain behavior. Some of this behavior is harmless, such as the response of reaching out your hand when someone offers theirs to shake. Other behavior can be problematic, such as overeating as a conditioned response to anxiety or sadness. Some of us inadvertently condition ourselves to obsess about our ex and feel heartbroken. Luckily, we can also condition ourselves to stop obsessing and install a new habit that makes us feel better.

REIMAGINING YOUR EX

Think about your ex now. As soon as you remember what someone looks like, you are using visualization. Recall what they looked like. What are
they wearing? What is the expression on their
face? What are they doing? Where is the picture
of them located relative to you? Is it in front of
you, or to the left or the right? Is it life size or
smaller? Is it a movie or is it a still image? Is it
solid or is it transparent? Do you hear their voice?
Now, as you keep seeing them in your mind's
eye, notice the feelings that arise in you. Make
a note of those feelings.

Now you could remember or imagine them
differently. In your mind you can be the greatest
ever film director. You can reshoot the scenes of
your memory and imagination in any way you

want. You can change the action, soundtrack, lighting, camera angles, framing, focus, speed—all the variables are up for grabs.

So now let's change how you are visualizing your ex and notice how it affects your feelings.

1. Bring to mind the picture you had of them.

2. Notice where it appears and how big it is.

3. Now drain the color out until it looks like an old black and white picture.

4. Move the image further and further away until it is a tenth of its original size.

5. Shrink it even further, right down to a little black dot.

6. Notice how your feelings have changed and compare how you feel now to the note you made earlier.

THE POWER OF IMAGINATION

Years of using hypnosis and the psychology of personal change have proved to me that without a shadow of doubt habits and imagination are far more powerful than logic and willpower. For example, ask yourself to feel wonderful now. Does that make a difference? Now imagine winning millions of dollars in a lottery and having your favorite movie star ask you to work on a special project with them. Go on, really imagine it vividly, with full color, sound and action. Take your time. Now, isn't that a bit different from just asking yourself to feel wonderful?

Your body responds far more to the vivid use of imagination than to a simple command. In fact, the human nervous system cannot tell the difference between a real and a vividly imagined experience. **What you rehearse over and over again in your mind conditions you.** When you imagine something repeatedly you make it easier for the brain to automate it. This is why athletes visualize winning over and over again to achieve their peak performances. When you first learned to read, you had to do it consciously and deliberately. Then, after you had done it for a while, you stored the ability in your unconscious mind and now you do it automatically without thinking.

Heartbreak is partly something that happens to us, but it is also an upset we maintain by making certain pictures and saying certain things to ourselves over and over again. It's as though we hypnotize ourselves to feel bad.

Why some people don't experience heartbreak and others do

With all that going on, you might ask yourself, how come some people don't feel heartbroken? The people who don't experience heartbreak at the end of a relationship have already left emotionally. Often they already have someone else to go to, a "better" future already planned. They have thought about it over and over again and reinforced the neural pathways so that their new, exciting future feels very real. The old relationship is coded very differently in their minds. They see it as a piece of history to which they are no longer attached. This explains why the length of a relationship is not always equal to the amount of upset at the end. It's the future-planning you do, whether conscious or unconscious, that determines your attachment to a person. The pain you feel in heartbreak is proportionate to the meaning you made from the future that's been cancelled.

All day long your conscious mind is thinking, processing your awareness and registering your feelings. Whatever it does repeatedly gets transferred to the automatic processes of the unconscious mind. Every thought you think has the potential to change your feelings. At a physical level all the activity of the conscious and the unconscious mind is manifest as electrical impulses in the brain and the production and modification of the special chemicals called "neuropeptides" that organize and control your body chemistry.

At this level being heartbroken is simply creating the body chemistry and neurological states that are coded as "unhappy." So one way to understand mending your broken heart is that it is instructing your body not to make that particular neurobiological state anymore but to make a new, more comfortable one instead. We can do this by carefully redirecting the way we make the pictures and soundtrack in our head. It is not that the pictures by themselves are powerful, it is the fact that the meaning we give them is reflected in our neurology and body chemistry. That is why changing the pictures and frames we use in our heads has such a powerful effect on our feelings.

FALLING IN AND OUT OF LOVE

Over the last few years I have had a lot of fun and learned a great deal from working with Richard Bandler, the creative genius behind Neuro-Linguistic Programming, often known as NLP. NLP is a practical approach which makes use of the way the mind operates to make it work for us, instead of letting it carry on with whatever habits or patterns it has picked up on our journey through life. Richard made an important discovery a few years ago about how human beings fall in and out of love.

When someone is in love they are fully associated in their happy memories; that is, they see their memories from the inside, from the point of view they had at the time. When they think of the bad times they are dissociated; that is, they see what happened as if they were standing outside and looking at themselves, as though it were someone else. So the good times have more emotional intensity and the bad times have less. That reinforces the good feelings they have in relation to their lover, and they feel in love. Regularly thinking about loving reinforces the neural pathways in the brain that create those feelings in the mind and body.

However, when someone falls out of love, they flip the pictures in their head round the other way and *dissociate* themselves whenever they think of happy memories with their partner. They see those memories from the outside, and look at themselves as though looking at someone else. Next they associate into all the bad times and vividly remember them from the inside. Put simply, they step out of the good times and into the bad. This has the effect of changing their feelings.

HOW TO FALL OUT OF LOVE

Part of being heartbroken is still feeling in love with how your ex used to be. It hurts because part of you is still attached to your ex. Now I am going to show you how to help that part of you release itself from those painful feelings.

1. Recall five times you felt very in love with your ex and make a list of them, so you can easily call them to mind in a moment.

2. Start to recall the first memory again, then step out of it and move the image of that event away from you so that you can see yourself in the picture. Move the image away until it is small and the emotional intensity is reduced.

3. Drain out the color so that it is black and white, then make it transparent. When you look at the event like this it will seem like it is happening to someone else and the emotional

intensity will be further reduced. By changing these variables you are recoding the memory.

4. When you've finished recoding the first memory, do the same with the next memory.

5. Work through them all until you have done all five.

6. Next, spend some time remembering in detail five negative experiences with your ex-partner, where you felt very definitely un-attracted to them. Think of the times when they did something that really hurt you, turned you off or offended you. Find five and make a list of them so you can easily call them to mind.

7. Now take the least appealing memory and *fully* return to that moment. Go back and run through it all over again. Step into the memory so that you are seeing the things you saw, hearing the things you heard and fully feeling the things you felt all over again.

8. Now turn up the color and the clarity. Make the memory as bright and clear as you can and feel the feelings getting stronger and stronger.

9. Go through each of the other four memories of when you were not attracted to your ex-partner, and step into them, seeing what you saw, hearing what you heard and feeling how you felt. Carry on until you feel you have had quite enough of them and even the idea of thinking about them is totally unattractive.

Take your time over the exercise. Concentrate and do it methodically and carefully. Some people have found that doing this just once makes them feel totally different. Other people like to do it every day. To make sure the effect sticks, do it every day for two weeks. Each repetition will strengthen the neural pathways you create, so it gets easier and quicker until the feeling becomes automatic.

3

WHAT IS THE POINT
OF THESE FEELINGS?

We have seen how we can change our feelings by modifying the pictures we make in our minds. So surely we should now be able to change any feelings we want with just a few applications of those techniques. No more problems! All my feelings under control! Well, sometimes, for some people, it can be that simple. When there are no complications, you really can feel better that fast. For many of us, however, there can be a few more things to sort out.

You may have found that as you practiced the techniques in the last chapter you did feel better, but that you also had some kind of sense or idea that there was something missing, or something else to do. If that is what you felt, you are right. If you didn't feel that, you are right, too. In both cases you would be right because your emotions are part of your intelligence. They are not just sensations that float around your life. Emotions are ways of saying, "Pay attention to this." If you are feeling bad, it is because there is something you need to notice. **Meeting and understanding our painful feelings is how we learn and grow as people.**

To understand what to do, how your emotions work and how to interpret them correctly, we are going to take a look at what emotions are, how they can help us and when they can be misleading.

EMOTIONS

Psychologist Paul Ekman famously demonstrated that all human beings share a fundamental set of emotions by showing that people from different cultures express the same emotions when given the same stimulus. He showed that these emotions, which he called "basic emotions," are innate: that is, they are built-in. They are hardwired; they are not learned. The basic emotions include joy, distress, fear, surprise, anger and disgust. All humans are capable of feeling these emotions and we all recognize the facial expressions that are characteristic of them. These emotions are simple responses that help us to navigate life and learn from our experiences. We learn quickly to avoid things that give rise to fear and disgust and to move towards things that bring us joy.

There is another set of emotions, called by psychologists "higher cognitive emotions," which includes love, pride, embarrassment, shame, guilt, jealousy and envy. Higher cognitive emotions differ from basic emotions. They are also universal but they are triggered and expressed differently in different cultures. What they have in common is that they all pertain to personal relationships. In other words, to feel a higher cognitive emotion, you have to have some *relationship* to someone else.

You can feel fear on your own, you can feel disgust on your own, but you cannot feel embarrassment without being aware of someone else's point of view. Another person does not have to be present. You can feel embarrassed or ashamed all on your own in an empty room. But you can only feel those emotions because of the existence of other people and their expectations. Similarly, there must be someone else involved to feel love or jealousy or envy. In other words, *all the higher cognitive emotions tell us something about how we are relating to other people.*

Relating to other people is a fundamental part of being human. The better we are at it, the more easily we realize our ambitions and the more we enjoy the relationships we have. In fact, the better we manage our relationships the more successful we are in every aspect of life. Understanding our emotions, or "emotional intelligence," is the key to improving our relationships.

CARL JUNG

Carl Jung, one of the founding fathers of psychotherapy, spent many years investigating the human psyche. He meticulously noted and analyzed his own experience, both in life and in his dreams. He traveled from Europe to Africa, India and America seeking people and experiences to deepen his understanding of the human condition. In New Mexico he met a Native American chief called Ochwiay Biano and had a conversation with him that struck him so powerfully he remembered it ever after. He wrote it down many years later in his autobiographical book, *Memories, Dreams, Reflections*.

"See," Ochwiay Biano said, "how cruel the whites look. Their lips are thin, their noses are sharp, their faces furrowed and distorted by folds. Their eyes have a staring expression; they are always seeking something. What are they seeking? The whites always want something; they are always uneasy and restless. We do not know what they want. We do not understand them. We think that they are mad."

I asked him why he thought the whites were all mad. "They say that they think with their heads," he replied.

"Why, of course. What do you think with?" I asked him in surprise.

"We think here," he said, indicating his heart.

Chief Biano opened Jung's eyes to the limitations of Western "rational" thinking. Our lives are not valuable because they are rational, and decisions are not good because they are logical. Our actions are wise and our lives are rich when we are guided by a sense of value that is rooted in our hearts, in the wisdom of our emotions, and not merely in the rationality of our heads. In fact, Jung came to believe, along with many other great thinkers, that in modern life we often behave in a back-to-front way. We make rationality the judge of what we should do and feel, rather than letting our feelings guide how we use our capacity for logic. What Chief Biano knew, modern psychotherapists have rediscovered. **If we work with our emotions we can reach a wisdom that is more personal and more accurate than the intelligence of our intellect alone.**

This does not mean that emotions are infallible guides to action. Far from it. To reach the wisdom of our emotions we must work with them. We have to be careful to remember that we experience a huge range of feelings—just as great a range as we have of thoughts. Some of our thoughts are trivial and stupid; others are profound. It is the same with feelings: some are trivial, others profound. Discrimination at the level of feelings is as important as being able to think clearly and rationally. As we will see, it is important to get down to the essential core of our emotions.

Chief Biano was pointing to the source of our emotional intelligence, where we understand our deeper, wiser feelings. When we use our attention to unravel our feelings, we discover that they can lead us to a significantly richer understanding of ourselves, and hence a deeper understanding of the people around us.

EMOTIONAL LEARNING

Heartbreak is not just our emotions telling us that our relationship has ended. It is also our emotions telling us we need to look after ourselves, and, very importantly, that the beliefs we have held which caused these feelings are no longer appropriate for us.

Emotions are, if you like, our sixth sense. They are our feeling of living. They are our awareness of people, and they contain a subtle and important understanding of our relationships. Emotions change and evolve over time because we change and situations change as time passes. Sometimes our unconscious mind holds some emotions back until we are strong enough to face them. Equally, it never lets us experience an emotion we can't deal with—although there can be times when we find that difficult to believe!

Learning to handle our emotions and to understand them is a fundamental part of growing up, just like learning to use our minds to think clearly, or using our hands to write or draw or make things. Unfortunately, for the last three hundred years our culture has woefully undervalued this emotional education. Indeed, in many societies a high value has been placed on suppressing and ignoring emotional reactions. Imagine if we all agreed to ignore our ability to see things. It would make life twice as difficult. We would bump into each other and get lost all the time. This is exactly what we do when we suppress and ignore our emotions.

In the previous chapter we looked at how to deal with emotions arising from how we think about the past and how we imagine the future. However, some emotions arise from our real, immediate surroundings and from the process of change that is going on inside us. These emotions have valuable lessons to teach us. In this chapter we will look at how to learn from these emotions. At this point, people ask me one of two questions. The first is "How can I tell the difference between emotions that are just reactions to the pictures in my head and emotions that have an important message I can learn from?"

The answer is simple. If an emotion is unimportant or no longer truly relevant to your life, it vanishes when you change the pictures in your head. If it is important and relates to a real, current situation you need to learn from, it will come back, because it will be triggered by your experience. If changing the pictures is not enough, there is something in the real world to deal with. When the emotion turns up, you need to notice it and learn from it. As to how to do that, read on.

The second question people ask is "If emotions are so great, and they can teach us so much, how come they can be such a problem?" The answer to this is a little longer. Essentially, emotions are not foolproof. There are five situations that cause us to experience our emotions as problems:

• First, as we have seen in the previous chapter, we can have emotions about pictures in our head and the things we say to ourselves. We are not responding to real life, but to memories or habitual thought patterns.

• Second, as we will see in chapter 5, we may have inherited negative emotional patterns that repeat themselves automatically.

• Third, we can confuse feelings with facts.

• Fourth, we can have feelings about our feelings.

• Fifth, we get confused by the timing of our emotions, so we don't react properly to what they are telling us.

We will look at the last three now, and see how to process our feelings so that we can learn from them.

FACTS AND FEELINGS

"I'll never find a person like her again." "He was the only man I could ever love." We have all heard statements like that. You may even have thought or said something like it yourself. Is it a fact? Or a feeling?

You can't prove that you will never meet a certain type of person any more than you can prove that it won't rain tomorrow. It isn't the sort of thing you can prove. It isn't a matter of logic. So it is not a logical fact.

But that sort of comment doesn't even begin to dent the conviction of someone who says this. No rational argument about what you can and can't prove is going to make a difference here. Actually, it is very likely on a planet with 6 billion people that you will find another person, sooner or later, who touches you as deeply and probably loves you more fully. But, again, probability is not at all persuasive to many people. If you say, "He was the only man I could ever love," you really feel it is true. What is going on?

The truth is hinted at above—you *feel* it is true. This statement is a feeling disguised as a fact. You cannot know that you will never meet another person as good or even better. You cannot know that you will never fall in love with another person. You cannot know that it is true any more than you can prove it is false. But why would anyone treat such a feeling as a fact?

The answer is that part of us is desperate for certainty. Deep down we all know that feelings are changeable. And that is very hard to live with, when feelings change from ones you enjoy to ones that make you miserable. Part of us doesn't want to admit it is over. We don't want to accept that our ex's feelings have changed now, and we don't want to accept the uncertainty facing our own feelings.

We hide feelings as facts precisely because deep down we know that they can be painful. Unfortunately, hiding them doesn't change them. As we shall see, it is by accepting our feelings, however painful they are, and turning towards them that we learn from them, and then, as if by magic, the pain dissolves.

FEELINGS ABOUT FEELINGS

Our conscious mind allows us to think about ourselves. As philosopher Charles Taylor puts it, "We are self-interpreting animals." Hence we have the ability to have feelings about our feelings. This capacity to have feelings about our feelings has made possible an entire history of suffering.

When you are heartbroken the simple fact is that you feel bad because a relationship has ended. You want what you can't have. But for many of us, that is not the end of it. We might feel scared of feeling so bad, or angry about it. Some people feel scared that they may never stop feeling bad, or feel scared that they will never be happy enough to have another relationship, or feel ashamed of feeling so distraught. All these are feelings about the original feeling of heartbreak.

All these extra feelings add to the burden of heartbreak. And feelings about feelings can even be stronger than the original feeling. They amplify themselves. For example, you might be afraid that the bad feelings could just carry on and on. That fear is itself a bad feeling, and so it keeps you feeling bad for longer. So the extra feeling has brought about the very thing you were worried about. Feelings about feelings create loops that amplify themselves. Sometimes people think that the stronger the emotion the more valid or important it is. That is not necessarily true. Some feelings seem powerful simply because they have been amplified by feeding on themselves over and over again. They are not necessarily more true, nor more important. Becoming conscious of this effect breaks the cycle and destroys its power.

One of my clients was very caught up in feelings about her feelings and her case illustrated how debilitating this can be. When we first met, she said she simply did not know how to get through the day. She felt awful and was ashamed of herself for feeling so bad. Throughout her marriage her husband had put her down. He was rude about her looks, he belittled her job, he was never kind about anything she did. Then he left her. She felt her life was pointless. She said she must be heartbroken because she felt so bad about him leaving, even though living with him was awful too.

She was in despair. Despair is the feeling that anything you do and anything you feel is useless. While Maria was in despair I knew we would get nowhere if we discussed her feelings, or the reasons why she felt so bad. Instead I asked her to fantasize about what it would be like if she had managed to recover from her experiences, from the years of abuse and the shock of her husband leaving. What would she do? Where would she live? What sort of feelings would she have?

Maria immediately told me that she didn't believe she would ever recover. I didn't argue with her. I insisted that I was not talking about an actual recovery. I emphasized that I was not asking her to believe anything at all. I was simply asking her to imagine an alternative reality in which she had managed to get over her ex. What would her behavior be like then? What would her feelings and desires be? What sort of things would she do, and what sort of things might happen to her?

Maria played along very halfheartedly at first. It was difficult to imagine such a different world. We started talking about very small changes such as maybe recovering her appetite or paying more attention to her appearance. Then I asked her to let rip with her imagination, and think of the most extraordinarily different and happy Maria she could possibly imagine.

Gradually she became interested in this alternative reality and little by little she invented more and more positive happenings.

Eventually she decided she would feel proud of herself. She would probably change her job and probably start dating or flirting with other men. We explored this new reality for nearly an hour and then I asked Maria how she felt. She felt far, far better. Her body had naturally responded to the positive scenes she was imagining.

I asked Maria to spend twenty minutes every evening imagining that alternative reality in which she had recovered from her relationship. When she came back the following week she confessed that she had actually spent hours at a time exploring her alternative reality. She told me that she had now changed her mind. She believed that she would get over the breakup of her marriage, and she already felt different about it. What was more, during the last week she had forgotten about her ex for hours at a time.

Maria had put up with her husband's abuse for far too long because she had ignored her own feelings, which

Alternative Future

As we saw in the previous chapter, the body responds to vivid imagination just as if it were reality. So if you could do with a lift right now, do exactly what Maria did.

1. Imagine there is a corridor in front of you. Imagine walking down it, away from the present towards a door.

2. Open the door, and see beyond it a world in which you have totally recovered from your heartbreaking relationship.

3. See what you look like, what you wear, where you go, who you see.

4. Now step into this new world and into the new happy you. Vividly imagine the whole experience from the inside, seeing what you would see, hearing what you would hear and feeling how good and happy you feel.

It is not a matter of believing in it—just imagine it, as vividly as possible. While the whole process of healing is going on this is a fabulous way to give yourself a boost, helping yourself with every second you do it.

were telling her very clearly it was wrong. Once she had recovered from her despair, Maria's therapy was to learn to respect her feelings rather than treat them as problems.

POSITIVE INTENTIONS

I used a different technique with a man who came to see me after he split up with his wife. Robert didn't say he felt heartbroken; he said he just couldn't get the picture of her having sex with another guy out of his head. The picture made him feel angry about his ex and distrustful of his new girlfriend.

I decided to use an old-fashioned, but nevertheless effective, approach called Parts Therapy. It lets us assume that we have individual aspects of our psyche in charge of various parts of us. You could decide, for example, that there's a part in charge of your emotions, or of a particular aspect of your behavior, such as a phobia. You hear people use this way of thinking about their psyche when they say something like "Part of me wants to go to the cinema and part of me wants to stay at home." Some psychologists behave as if these parts actually exist as separate entities, and devise lists, categories and clinical names for them. It is important to remember they are constructs. Constructs are ways of thinking we make up so that working with ideas or emotions is easier. The reason I used Parts work to describe an aspect of his psyche was that it allowed Robert to create a dialogue that could reveal more about his feelings.

I asked Robert to make up a picture of the part of him that was getting angry and distrustful. He imagined a large, powerful man who looked like a bodyguard so, to keep things simple, we decided to call him Mr. Body-guard. I asked Robert to point to where Mr. Bodyguard was and then I imagined him too, sitting in the room with us. Next I did something very important. I made the assumption that Mr. Bodyguard had a positive func-tion, that he was there to do something useful for Robert. I said to Robert, "I understand that Mr. Body-guard does something very important for you. Is that right?" He looked at where we were imagining Mr. Bodyguard to be and answered, "Yes." I asked him to imagine what he thought Mr. Bodyguard might say.

It might seem a bit weird that two adult men were sitting in a study imagining a positive part of someone and talking to it, but I have noticed that good therapy is mostly that, imagining something positive and engaging with it. I've also noticed that psychological suffering is mostly the opposite—imagining something negative and engaging with that.

Anyway, next I asked Robert to ask Mr. Bodyguard what he did for him. He answered, "He stops me getting too close to people."

"What does that get you?" I asked.

"It stops people hurting me," he replied.

"And what does that get you?" I asked.

"It keeps me safe."

"OK," I said. "So Mr. Bodyguard keeps you safe, he protects you."

"Yes," said Robert.

"Thank you, Mr. Bodyguard," I continued. "You fulfill a very important function for Robert. You protect him, and we want you to continue to do that. However, it seems to me that you have been overdoing your job. You've been showing him that picture to make sure he doesn't let it happen again, but unfortunately that is also keeping alive the feeling of resentment towards his ex-wife. It means Robert feels bad most of the time and doesn't trust his girlfriend."

Robert was nodding with agreement. I continued to talk to Mr. Bodyguard and asked him if he would find a way to carry on protecting Robert but also let him trust his girlfriend. I asked the Mr. Bodyguard part of Robert to take all the time he needed to search through Robert's memory and imagination to find a new way to do this, and when he had found it he was to nod Robert's head.

Soon Robert's head nodded and I asked him how he felt.

He thought about it and replied, "It feels like it's possible."

So I asked Mr. Bodyguard to let Robert imagine what it was going to be like to feel safe with his girlfriend without thinking of his ex. He sat back and relaxed and then he nodded and heaved a sigh. Eventually he said, "Yeah, it feels like a burden has lifted. I can imagine being with my girlfriend without the bad feeling, because that picture is a long way away. It is the size of a pinhead. I know it's there if I need it to remind me, but for now I can get on with things. I feel so much better." The Mr. Bodyguard part had moved the picture away in his imagination, so that he could look at it if ever he needed it, but for the rest of the time it was just a tiny little dot.

The important part of this story is not the Parts work. You don't have to be a skilled psychotherapist to use it. The most important thing I did for Robert was to share with him the simple assumption that **there is a positive intention at the root of all our feelings.**

Working with your feelings

An emotion is a bit like someone knocking on your door to deliver a message. If the message is urgent, it knocks loudly. If it is very urgent it knocks very loudly. If you don't answer the door, it knocks louder and louder and louder. It keeps knocking until you open the door. Then it delivers its message. As soon as you understand even part of it, it becomes part of your self-understanding. And that is part of your self. So you are changed, and the emotion does its job.

Working with your feelings is learning to use your emotional intelligence to the full. There is a whole world of understanding and insight available through your emotions. You can open them up almost endlessly to find more understanding and more feeling.

In heartbreak, because so much happens all at once, there is often a backlog of emotional learning to get through. But if you do just one bit at a time your uncon-scious mind will protect you, and give you a rest so that you can deal with the next bit when you are ready.

Robert's situation was a classic illustration of jealousy. He was making a picture in his head of something attractive to him and then saying to himself, "I can never have that again." Robert transformed his jealousy by finding out what it was trying to do for him. Instead of being preoccupied with his ex-wife, he learned how to change himself.

Exploring the meaning of feelings

To give you another example of how this works, I will tell you about another client, Mark. At first he was reluctant to admit what he was feeling at all. As he put it, he was "embarrassed even to be having emotions like this." I suggested we see what they were without prejudging them.

Mark wasn't sure whether he wanted to get back together with his ex or get even with her.

"What do you mean?" I asked.

He explained that his ex, Fiona, tended to choose what they did. Occasionally he would express a preference, but it always seemed to involve a great scene or an argument. In the end he would go along with her.

"Does that mean you ignored your own wishes?" I asked.

Mark looked a little embarrassed again and shrugged. "I suppose so."

I asked him to give me an example, as small and simple as possible.

FINDING THE POSITIVE INTENTION

This simple technique helps you to find the positive intention behind any bad feeling.

1. Clarify the emotion that you find painful or uncomfortable. Don't be distracted by thinking about the cause, just focus on the feeling. Notice where you feel it.

2. Next, ask yourself what the feeling is about. Let the answer come up in your mind. You might get an image, an idea or an intuition.

3. If it is about another feeling, ask yourself what that other feeling is about.

4. Keep going until you get to an original feeling about yourself. This is the reason that it matters to you.

5. Now ask yourself, What is the positive intention behind this original feeling?

6. Once you have identified that positive intention, and whatever it reveals that you need to know about yourself, focus on that and you will no longer need the negative emotion.

He told me about a time they had had some friends over. As he was putting on some music, she said, "No, not that." So he put on something else and she said, "Absolutely not." He felt slightly resentful at the time, but now they had split up it was the sort of thing that made him really angry to remember. He realized that Fiona had bullied him.

As he asked himself why it made him so angry, Mark saw that he was angry not only with her, but also with himself. He felt that he should have been more forceful. "The thing is," he exclaimed, "she just assumed she could take charge because I'd been such a wimp. And that's what annoys me!"

As the words burst from his mouth Mark seemed to become aware of what was bugging him. There was something in his own behavior, something for which he was responsible, that had been inviting Fiona to do whatever she wanted. We carried on exploring similar incidents and a pattern began to emerge.

Mark had never taken these incidents seriously; he saw them all as "trivial." But I pointed out that in life and relationships most of what we do could be called trivial. As a result, the way we do trivial things is important. Often what is most important is not the grand gestures but the little details of our daily life. As we talked, Mark realized he didn't need to feel foolish about his anger.

Fiona knew what she liked, and tended to state her preferences straight away, whereas Mark tended to take longer to make up his mind. He also thought of himself as a fairly easygoing type, so whenever Fiona leapt in with her choice, whether it was music or food or the color they painted the kitchen, he told himself it didn't matter. It was just one decision, and he was easygoing about little things.

Mark thought that his willingness to agree with her had been helping the relationship. Now he saw that the opposite was true. He didn't ask for what he wanted, so he never got his own way, and then he blamed Fiona.

He had also misunderstood himself. He had told himself he was easygoing. Of course, that was true some of the time, but not always. In other words, he had let his belief that he was easygoing override his feelings that were telling him something else.

"Actually," said Mark at the end of the session, "I was lazy. I knew that Fiona was a tough cookie, and I just ducked out by telling myself I was easygoing. I needed to confront her a lot more in order for us both to get what we needed from that relationship."

For Mark, working with the emotions he was ashamed of helped him to understand what had happened. His emotions were trying to tell him he needed to stand up for himself in the future. As he realized that, his anger dissolved and he let go of trying to get even, or get back, with Fiona.

Mark needed to get underneath the feelings he had about his feelings. When he worked his way back to what they were telling him about his relationship it helped him to move on. But as I mentioned earlier, there are times when the problem is not feelings about feelings. It is just a matter of timing.

The importance of timing

A young woman called Mandy, whose situation was a perfect illustration of the importance of timing, came to see me. Mandy could not explain her own behavior. All that she knew was that she couldn't seem to leave Charlie, even though he treated her badly.

Charlie was a moody and difficult boyfriend, and in the two years they had been together he had cheated on her continually. At first he was warm, witty and caring and Mandy felt head over heels in love. As the months passed, Charlie paid less and less attention to her, but from time to time he would become romantic and charming again, and she would feel herself love him all over again. She could never tell when he was going to be nice and when he was going to behave badly. Mandy was fascinated to discover that the unpredictability of his behavior was one of the key factors that made it so difficult for her to leave him.

B. F. Skinner, one of America's most famous psychologists, believed that our behavior, and that of other animals, is governed by a simple rule: If our behavior rewards us, we repeat it; if it doesn't, we don't. This explanation of human actions is called "behaviorism." It seems uncomplicated, but Skinner devised some ingenious experiments with rats that showed it could have curious consequences. He put rats into a box in which there was a lever. When the rats pressed the lever, they got food. The rats pretty soon learned to press the lever repeatedly to get more and more food.

Now comes the interesting bit. He changed the setup so that the rats were no longer fed on every click of the lever. In one box, the rats were fed regularly after a specific number of clicks. In another box, the rats were fed *intermittently,* after a random number of clicks.

When the rats had got used to the new conditions, he turned off the food supply entirely. After a while the rats in the first box stopped pressing the lever. The rats that had been fed intermittently kept on pressing the lever far, far longer.

The rats who were used to a regular reward soon worked out that it had stopped. However much they pressed the lever, they got no food. A hundred or so clicks convinced them that the mechanism was broken. But for the other rats, their experience of the random gaps between feeding meant they had no way of knowing that the food delivery system had stopped. Maybe they were just experiencing an unusually long break in the service. So they kept on trying.

Skinner called this effect the "law of intermittent reinforcement." A very clear example of the same phenomenon in humans is gambling. When you gamble, you win some and you lose some. The bets that win reward the behavior of betting. This is reinforcement. More bets are losers, which do not reinforce the behavior. However, the occurrence of winning bets is unpredictable and intermittent. In spite of the fact that overall the gambler is losing more bets and more money than he is winning, the intermittent nature of the reward renders the reinforcement particularly effective, because every time the gambler places a bet it might, it just might, win. He can never know for certain that it is not worth continuing. So he places just one more bet . . .

The same law worked for Mandy with Charlie. After the first month or so, she felt that Charlie wasn't behaving as though he really loved her, but at random intervals he would become warm and loving again. She kept hanging in there, and from time to time, just when she was about to give up, they would have a crisis, he would promise to mend his ways and for a little while everything would be lovely. Charlie's likeable behavior was intermittent and unpredictable. That reinforced her willingness to give him one more chance.

Intermittent reinforcement is so powerful that we overlook what is actually happening because what we want to happen might just do so at any moment. Mandy put up with Charlie's dreadful behavior for so long because she was always focusing on what might happen and ignoring her feelings about what he actually did.

BREAKING FREE

Richard Bandler has a friend who runs a shelter for women who have been abused by their partners. His friend couldn't find a way to persuade some of the women to stop giving their partners just one more chance. They went back and got abused again and again. Eventually one of the women was killed by her partner. That's when Richard was asked to help. He started by interviewing the women from the shelter who had successfully left abusive relationships. He wanted to find out what had taken place that allowed them to leave. He made a fascinating discovery. They all said something like "I kept thinking about all the bad things that happened, over and over again."

When these women thought about all the bad times over and over again, one after the other, the bad memories began to join up so that there wasn't any space between them. Previously the intermittent reinforcement of the occasional good times had kept them attracted. Then all the bad memories joined up until their cumulative effect broke the intermittent reinforcement. Now, whenever they thought of their ex, all they could remember was the abuse and pain and fear. They could no longer maintain any attachment to the idealized view they had of him. The bad feelings built up until the women reached a point where they could not reverse the process. One more bad experience was the straw that broke the camel's back. They couldn't think of their ex-partner in the same way again. They had crossed a threshold.

Richard decided to teach the other women in the shelter how to remember all the bad times joined together so that they could feel their full effect. The psychological mechanism that causes us to cross a threshold is in us all. When we have enough bad experiences close together we have to change. However, Richard decided the women in the shelter couldn't afford to wait months or even years for it to activate by itself. He showed them how to activate it immediately, before any further injuries.

This is the technique Richard created. Many of the people who have used it with me have said that it was the single most powerful action they took to free themselves from their attachment to an ex. They have said things like "I don't have any feelings towards my ex now." "I feel confident now. If I have any feelings of longing, I have a surefire way to get rid of them." "My ex feels like someone I used to know a long time ago." "OK, it's turned off the overwhelming feelings. I can handle it now."

The Threshold Technique

Part of the power of this technique comes from the speed at which you run it. It is important to take the time to read it through properly before you start. If you have to stop to figure out the next step, you will lose momentum. So decide now whether you are ready for a radical change in your feelings, and read it through carefully before you begin.

1. Call to mind a picture of yourself with your ex when you were in love. Look at it as though it was a photograph and notice how strongly it affects you now. Then just imagine putting it to one side so you can check it again in a moment.

2. Next call to mind four negative experiences with your ex-partner where you felt very definitely upset or repulsed by them. Perhaps you will think of times when they did something that really offended you or did something that you found hurtful. Make a list of them so you can easily call them to mind.

3. Now fully return to those four negative memories one at a time in detail as though you were inside each of them reenacting the moment. See the things you saw, hear the things you

heard and feel completely the negative feelings you felt all over again, like you are actually there.

4. Go through the memories again and again, one after another, each time making the images a bit bigger, brighter and more colorful, so they are more and more intense. Now go through them faster and faster, until the events are overlapping, until there is no break at all between all the worst parts happening over and over again.

5. When you have generated a really strong negative feeling throughout your body, look at that picture of yourself when you were in love with your ex, and notice how differently you feel now.

6. Finally imagine stepping out of all the memories and imagine all the pictures and feelings to do with your ex floating away from you and going off into the past.

Many people only need to do this technique once to feel totally free of their attachments to their old relationship. But if you want to, you can do it again carefully and thoroughly in order to reinforce the effect.

4

How do I cope
with my ex?

We've concentrated so far on what you do to heal your broken heart. And that is our most important focus. But for every relationship that breaks up there are two external factors to deal with: your ex, and all the people you know. As well as healing on the inside, you have to deal with what goes on around you.

When you split up, your ex doesn't usually evaporate into thin air. They might live in the same neighborhood or work in the same office. You might have friends in common or support the same team. If so, you have to cope with their presence in your life. Sometimes that's easy, sometimes it's not. In this chapter we're going to look at some of the reasons why your ex can be a difficulty in your life, and give you some key insights and tactics to stop you getting held back by them.

THE ME CLUB

My agent, Paul Duddridge, uses a brilliant metaphor to help you keep your boundaries in the right place. Imagine you were a club. Every club has rules. Nightclubs have rules, such as no fighting, no drugs or no under-21s. What are the rules of your club? What are the standards of behavior you expect from people you deal with? Would you let in liars? Or people who don't keep their word? Or people who don't return phone calls? Where do you draw the line?

What are your standards of politeness, kindness, reliability and honesty? Think about it now, and choose what sort of a club you would like to belong to. The club rules are the rules all your friends, partners and business acquaintances have to stick to.

Take a moment now and jot down the rules you want. Writing them down helps to clarify what you expect and what you will and won't tolerate. When you've written the rules, put them on the fridge or even next to the telephone. Your list will help you to keep a clear head and remind you of your principles if you get difficult phone calls from difficult people.

You don't have to tell anyone else about the club. These aren't the sort of rules that you enforce. You can't make anyone be honest or reliable if they don't want to. But if they don't follow the rules it means you don't let them in the club anymore. You don't have to have anything to do with them. If you don't make any arrangements with them, there is nothing they can let you down about.

It is very important to realize that the rules are rules for you too. You have to stick to them. If you don't, your behavior will signal to other people that they don't have to either, and the club will cease to exist. So if, for example, you think that people should not spread gossip, then that is one of the rules of your club. If you gossip, your behavior signals to the rest of the club that gossip is OK. The club won't last long.

The idea of the Me Club is very useful if you find yourself in situations where people are confusing you or pressurizing you and you don't know quite what to do. Ask yourself, "Would it be OK for a member of my club to do this?"

Equally, if your ex is behaving in a manner that hurts you or causes problems in your life, ask yourself, "Are they following the rules of my club?" If they are not following the rules, just withdraw. Stop talking to them. Stop seeing them. What they do outside your club is no concern of yours.

I have found this idea really useful. I got very annoyed with somebody who was making trouble in a company I was involved with and I began to try to work out how I could get my own back on them. I was getting more and more worked up, until my agent reminded me of the idea of the club. "Relax," he said. "They don't belong in your club anymore. You can be polite and just leave them behind." Suddenly it was a whole lot easier to see that person, knowing they were on the way out of my club.

Another time I discovered that a friend of mine was

saying unpleasant things about me behind my back. I took him aside and said, "I've heard what you've been saying, and I find it offensive. In fact, I'm hurt by it."

"Oh, I didn't mean it," he said. "Look, it is—"

"No," I interrupted. "Whatever you meant, I find it hurtful. Please don't do it anymore, and then we can remain friends."

I love the idea of the club, but it won't solve every problem. Many problems do not lend themselves to such clear-cut solutions. There can be complications. Sometimes people seem to be polite and reasonable and yet somehow you feel there is something dubious going on. In what follows we will look at situations that arise when people who have split up still have to deal with each other, but want to avoid getting hurt or abused.

"My ex relies on me"

In relationships partners often help each other out by doing jobs for each other. One might do the accounts, while the other looks after the car. This trading also happens on an emotional level. One day he'll boost her confidence, the next day she'll do the same for him. Doing jobs for one another, both practical and emotional, becomes one of the habits of a relationship. A classic example is a partnership where one person is a worrier and the other never worries at all. The worrier is always on the alert and sees problems coming a mile off. The other one can relax because someone is always looking out for them.

However, some people don't want to stop using the

arrangement just because the relationship has broken up. These are the exes who ring up and "just want a talk" when they feel bad, or want to pick out the parts of the relationship that are still useful to them even though they are no longer with their partner. It doesn't help you to move on if you keep getting drawn into being used.

If you have children or a business in common you can't help having a lot to do with each other. Children still require 100 percent of your love, but they should never be an excuse for your ex to exploit you. If you find yourself surrounded by complicated reasons, excuses and plans, or hear yourself justifying your actions to your friends or to yourself, pause for a moment, step back, and ask yourself, "Am I being taken advantage of?"

You might have to set some limits. You need to work out where to draw the line, and there are two questions you can ask yourself to clarify what is happening and where that line should be.

The first question is "When I come away from seeing my ex, who do I feel is running my life?" Always adjusting your plans to suit your ex, or always feeling bad after seeing them, are alarm bells warning you to set firmer limits. The second question is "If I had a good friend who was in a situation just like this, what advice would I give them?" Because of all the history you have with your ex, it is difficult for you to be objective. Imagining a good friend in the same situation is an easy way to get a more straightforward view of what is going on.

These questions allow you to step back and look at yourself in the bigger picture without being overwhelmed by your emotional involvement.

SETTING LIMITS

If you decide you need to set some limits on what you should do for your ex, here are three useful hints.

1. First, write down how much you will do and when you will stop. Doing this helps you to clarify exactly what you are prepared to do. It also helps to imprint it more firmly in your memory. You are more likely to remember and stick to decisions you write down than ones you only make in your head.

2. Second, stick to your plan, even if after you've made it you don't feel pressurized anymore. When someone senses their old tactics are not working, they often change and try something else. If they were using emotional blackmail,

they might suddenly start being super-
reasonable and then ask for something so
nicely that you are tempted to go along with it.
Don't. Don't get suckered into helping out
again just because they behave differently.
Stick to your plan for at least a month before
you even think of reviewing it.

3. Third, don't explain yourself. Just do what you
   think is reasonable and no more. Whenever
   any relationship has become difficult and
   manipulative, explanations only open the
   door to arguments, discussions and more
   complications. We will see more examples
   of this below. In the meantime, stick to your
   plan, do what you are prepared to do, don't
   get drawn into discussions, be polite and
   then leave.

Sex with your ex

Sometimes it goes further. Your ex tries to sleep with you. They don't want to get back together with you, they just want sex. Sex with your ex is never simple. Sex is a very powerful force. It bypasses the rationalizations and promises of the conscious mind and affects your emotions directly. Don't underestimate it.

Sexual attraction can be used to wield power. It can be used to control people. Anger, suffering and revenge can be expressed through sex. Some people hide from the complexity of their feelings by throwing themselves into the sensations of sex.

Not all sex is loving (and, just as importantly, not all loving is sexual). If you are heartbroken, it is your heart that needs healing, not your lust. Hard though it may be, it is worth refraining from sex with your ex. One question can help you both do that. Ask yourself, "Is sex all I want?" If sex is all you want, your ex is not the best person to get it from. Remember one of you is heartbroken, so the chances are that your ex doesn't feel the same way. They are about to spring a whole load of complications on you. If you just want sex, then both of you will get simple sex far more easily with someone else.

If sex is not all you want, what else do you want? If it is control, or an expression of anger or anything negative, be as honest as you can and say so. That will change the atmosphere pretty quickly. If what you want as well as sex is love, admit that to yourself. You don't have to say it to your ex. Admit it to yourself, because real love is one of the few things more powerful than sex, and focusing on it will stop you being pushed about by your hormones.

Love lasts longer than lust so wait for a better time when your hormones aren't raging and then talk. If your ex doesn't want to see you except when they want sex, then sex is all they want. That is a good reason for them being your ex.

If they want something more than sex, if they genuinely want you two to get back together, the big challenge for both of you is communicating honestly about what caused you to split up and taking responsibility for changing it. That takes time and patience and courage and clarity. Sexual hormones rushing round your bloodstream do not promote patience or clarity.

If sex happens, you'll know the complications it causes so don't add to them by beating yourself up. Forgive yourself, but remember what happened before the sex. Don't get into that situation again. If it happened when you got drunk with your ex, it is not enough to avoid getting drunk with them. Avoid the situation that led to you getting drunk together. Don't just avoid temptation, avoid the times and places where temptation hangs out.

"My ex is playing games"

There is a never-ending list of games that people play and tricks that people get up to. All the games are based, one way or another, on fear and insecurity.

People can act wounded or hurt, or blame you, or spread lies about you, or dangle in front of you the possibility of getting back together again. They can ring you up and ask to meet you and then tell you all about their new girlfriend or boyfriend. They can dump you and then get jealous if they see you with someone else. They may do all these things without meaning to be hurtful or difficult. This sort of behavior rarely comes from conscious or deliberate malevolence. Nine times out of ten it is simply the result of someone feeling lost or scared, or avoiding responsibility for their own emotions. Unconsciously they want to keep you in a game with them, even if it is not comfortable, because they are getting your attention and not facing their fears of moving on.

I won't try to write out a full list of all these games because I'm sure I'd never finish it. People can always come up with a new twist on an old idea. Instead let's look at what underlies all of them. The essence of these games is that they attempt to catch you off guard by using your automatic responses.

Social conditioning

There is a set of informal rules to which we all tacitly agree. It's social conditioning. For example, we tend to abide by conventions such as not talking during the show at a theatre, or asking permission before smoking in someone's house. If someone offers to shake your hand, you normally offer your hand without thinking.

We try to be polite to each other, and we don't normally tell lies. Another very powerful piece of conditioning is to reply as best we can when asked a question.

We don't think about these conventions much; we just tend to stick to them and it makes society tick along happily enough. However, the fact that we don't think about them means that these conventions are unconscious and can be used to string us along in ways we would not normally choose.

Even a simple question can be a trap. The most common way questions can be used against you is when there is an assumption buried in the question. Unless you are very careful, by answering the question you implicitly accept the assumption.

Salespeople, for example, are very good at asking questions that are difficult for you to answer without being drawn in the direction they want you to go. A car salesperson will ask, "Which color car do you prefer, the red or the blue?" The assumption he has slipped into this question is that you are interested in either of his cars in the first place. When several of these assumptions are strung together, they become even more persuasive. It is so difficult to keep track of them all that some of them slip through unchallenged, particularly if the conversation gets heated, such as with an ex.

"Are you going to sort out the house this week or leave it until next month?" It sounds like a simple question, and it is. It has simply assumed that you, not your ex, not the pair of you, not your lawyers and not anybody else but you, is going to sort out the house. The question about when it will be done has been used to disguise the assumption that it is up to you to do it.

The best defense is not even to try to spot all the assumptions and reject them. The best tactic is to learn to override your natural tendency to answer a question when it is asked. Learn to duck. There are three simple ways to do this.

The first way is one you can see demonstrated by politicians on the television any day of the week. A politician never answers a question directly. I once offered a member of Parliament a cup of tea. He was so programmed to be a politician that he couldn't just say yes. It took him five minutes to say that he thought under the circumstances that it was probably a good idea. So take a leaf out of the politician's handbook and answer a question you don't trust with a meaningless phrase and then go on to say what you want. For example: "I don't know about that, but what I think should be done is . . ."

The second way is to be noncommittal. Say something, but put off giving an answer: "I don't really know. I don't feel in a position to make a decision right now." "Well, I'm not sure, I'd have to think about that." "I'm not sure I'm the right person to answer that." And so on.

Thirdly, ask a question about the question: "What makes you ask that?" "How do you think I should respond?" "Is that the right way to put it?" "Do you think this is the right time to try to answer such a question?" And so on.

Of course, you don't have to answer questions at all. You can say nothing, or simply change the subject.

There may be serious issues to sort out with your ex. If you have property or children together you will need to answer questions. But you don't have to do so face-to-face. If you find that simple questions lead to manipulation, arguments and complications, ask your ex to put all their important questions in writing and give them or send them to you. Take your time to consider them on your own. Let your emotional reactions come out, and then when you have calmed down, decide on your reply. Put your answers in writing and send them back.

RELIABILITY

Reliability is a good thing isn't it? Not always. I was taught a very good lesson by an ex who was spectacularly unreliable. The relationship had been quite a roller-coaster ride. Looking back on it now I realize neither of us had a clue what was going on. She would be passionate and loving and then disappear for days on end. Throughout the relationship I was as reliable as could be. I thought that would help her to settle, rather than throw herself at me and then disappear. I don't think she saw it that way. I think she thought I was getting more and more boring.

Even after we split up she would still reappear in my life, offering love and demanding attention, and then disappear again. Eventually I got it. As long as I was patient, reliable and willing to accept her behavior, it would carry on happening. My willingness and reliability made it possible. I had a choice. I could become unreliable and find out if there was anything else in the relationship that would bring it back to life, or I could carry on and never know when she would turn up and throw my life upside down again. I let myself become just a little bit unreliable, and I didn't hear from her again.

There is nothing wrong with reliability at all. But if you don't want to be used, don't give it away for free to somebody who never gives it back.

GETTING DRAWN INTO A FIGHT

Have you ever intended to have a short, simple conversation with your ex and ended up in a slanging match? Have you ever wondered how that happened? And how it happened so fast?

As the saying goes, they pressed your buttons. Your ex knows what winds you up—the things you are sensitive about. When they press your buttons you defend yourself and it escalates. The most common form of defense is attack, so nine times out of ten we defend by attacking, and end up in a slanging match.

The strange thing is that other people often know our buttons better than we do ourselves. This is because our defenses are automatic. We don't want to feel whatever it is we are sensitive about, so we don't pay attention to it—we go straight on the attack.

Calm Anchor Technique

Here is a powerful strategy for avoiding a fight. The more you practice it, the easier it will be to use it when you need it. It is a very good idea to practice it, especially if your ex has had a lot of practice at provoking you. The more often you have been provoked, the more the pattern has been imprinted—so you need to imprint your alternative.

1. Remember a time when you felt calm, confident and in control of your feelings. See what you saw, hear what you heard and feel how you felt.

2. When that feeling of being calm, collected and keeping your cool is very strong, squeeze your thumb and middle finger together. This is called creating an anchor. You are associating this squeeze of your fingers in this particular way with this feeling of calm.

3. Relax your fingers and then do it again. Vividly remember a time you felt really calm and confident and then squeeze your thumb and finger together again in exactly the same way. Repeat this process five times.

4. Now, seeing yourself as though you were

watching someone else, remember a time when your ex provoked you. Looking back on it now and feeling quite separate from the situation, work out what you would rather have done in that situation instead of getting upset. You might have walked away, or laughed, or just been casual. Think about it for a while until you have a clear idea of how you could have handled the situation better.

5. Now go back to the beginning of the incident and this time remember it from the inside, seeing what you saw then and hearing what you heard then, and go through it until you sense the tension or annoyance beginning to build inside you.

6. As soon as you recognize the very beginning of that feeling of tension, squeeze your thumb and middle finger together just like you did before, and remember the feeling of staying calm and confident.

7. Now, keeping that feeling of calm, see the scene continuing and vividly imagine things going exactly the way you want. Imagine the scene from the inside, seeing what you see and hearing what you hear as though you are there, and feeling calm, confident and in control.

8. Next time you see your ex, at the first hint of any upset or irritation with them, squeeze your thumb and middle finger together in exactly the same way and remember that powerful feeling of cool, calm confidence.

As you practice this over and over again, you will find that it becomes easier and more powerful. This technique teaches your unconscious to create new neural pathways corresponding to a new response to your ex. It directs your wound-up feelings to move straight to an experience of calm and feeling good about yourself. When you practice this over and over and over again, you are rehearsing this transition, from beginning to feel angry to feeling calmly in control. Practice this as often as you need to until you can instantly access this calm, whenever you need it. The next time your ex tries to wind you up, press your thumb and middle finger together and you will easily stay calm, collected and in control and you will deal with the situation to your satisfaction. After a while you will find the pathways have become so strong that you don't even need to use the thumb-to-finger anchor to feel calm and in control. Just remembering that you can stay in control will enable you to do it.

Never explain

Some of my clients say to me, "If only my ex would understand, I would feel so much better." They are probably right, but there again, if their ex was willing to understand maybe the relationship wouldn't have ended. When things are going wrong, we have to accept that they are not necessarily going to go wrong in the right way. They might go wrong in the wrong way, as far as you are concerned.

Your ex will not necessarily understand or sympathize with you. The chances are that if you try to explain anything, or get them to understand your point of view, they will twist your words and misunderstand you. You simply can't make other people see things your way if they don't want to.

Tell the truth to your friends. Talk to them about how unreasonable your ex is. But don't expect your ex to admit you are right, even if you are. **Part of letting go is learning to live with the misunderstanding, the incompleteness and the messiness of it all.**

Nobody is perfect

You don't have to pretend you are invulnerable. Your emotions and your hopes are as valuable and important as anyone else's. If you lose a future you had hoped for, it is a real loss and it is right to grieve. You matter enough for this to hurt. You also matter enough to make it worth getting over that hurt, but if you feel sad, don't be ashamed to admit it. **If you admit your sadness to yourself, other people can't manipulate you by threatening to expose it.** People who hide from their own sadness do not grieve it and do not move on. Worse still, they become desperately attached to the facade of happiness they have created to hide behind, and end up spending all their energy protecting that facade. Nobody is perfect. We all make mistakes and we are all vulnerable.

Equally, we all have our own strengths. And, so long as they don't interfere with other people's liberties, your wishes and interests are just as good as anyone else's. There is no need for self-doubt or putting yourself down. And there is no need to pretend to be perfect or put on a mask. Who you are is absolutely fine.

However, you will find that some people do pretend they are invulnerable, they are not at all hurt, and everything in their life is just perfect. If anyone is pretending to you that they are perfect, or their life is perfect, don't let it wind you up. They are lying. Ask yourself why they do it. Why do they have to put on a show that they have no problems at all? Maybe they are frightened to admit it; maybe they are ashamed. Maybe they value their public face more than the truth of their emotions. Whatever their reasons, remember it is their problem, not yours.

If you pretend to your ex that you are perfect, you are lying—and they could use that against you. You don't have to be perfect. You can make mistakes; you can admit you are vulnerable. Don't get lured into pretending you are anyone other than yourself. If, for example, you want to get back with your partner and you don't acknowledge that to yourself, you could find yourself being used.

I had a client named Pete who split up with his girl-friend, Lois, because they were spending too much time fighting. As they had both agreed to separate, Pete couldn't understand why he was feeling so cut up. I asked him if he still saw Lois. It turned out that she kept calling him. She would ask for help or advice about some little thing, or suggest they met up for a coffee and a chat.

Pete would go along with it and help her or meet up, but he felt he was getting mixed messages. Lois would tell him how much she loved him, and then tell him about her problems with her new partner. Lois wanted to have Pete's support and friendship without admitting that she wanted it.

When we looked into how Pete felt about it, it be-came clear that secretly he was hoping they would be able to get back together. He saw that he was saying yes to Lois, but not admitting to himself (or to her) what he really wanted. He wasn't making an all-out effort to get the relationship going, but he wasn't leaving it behind. He was just hanging around, and Lois could use him for whatever help or support she wanted.

Pete needed to be truthful to himself. He needed to stand up for his wish to get back together and make it happen, or give up entirely. As long as he stayed in no man's land he was not going to move on—and he was not going to get Lois back either.

"Why do I feel unsure when I see my ex, even though I ended it?"

For most of us, most of the time, things that are difficult to get are more attractive than things that are readily available. There is a simple reason for this. If things are desirable, they are in demand, which makes them scarce, so scarcity becomes shorthand for desirability in the unconscious mind. In his fascinating book *Influence: Science and Practice,* Robert Cialdini summarized a series of experiments that demonstrate how availability and scarcity influence our judgment. In one experiment, several two-year-old boys were given the choice of two toys to play with. When one of the toys was significantly more difficult to get at, all the boys chose to go and play with it first. Well, that's just little boys, you might think. But other research showed that the same tendency is active in adults. A study in Colorado showed that teenage couples fell more deeply in love when their parents disapproved or interfered. When the parental interference reduced, so too did the romantic feelings.

In another experiment, the participants were asked to rate the quality of some cookies. Some people were offered a cookie from a jar containing two, and others were offered a cookie from a jar containing ten. Those who chose from two cookies consistently rated their cookie as better quality than those who were able to choose from ten. Why were the two-cookie choosers more satisfied? Simply that if there are only two cookies the unconscious mind automatically assumes that cookies are in short supply. Things that are desirable are usually in short supply, so the unconscious makes the plausible, though not strictly logical, assumption that these cookies are desirable. The scarcity principle is at work. But Stephen Worchel, the psychologist who devised the experiment, thought there might be more to discover, so he made a small variation to the procedure.

Some people saw a jar of ten cookies, but before they had tasted one the jar was removed and replaced with a jar containing two cookies. Then, like the other participants, they were offered one and asked to rate its quality. These participants rated the cookie more highly than those who had seen only two cookies. In other words, when the participants saw the cookies rapidly becoming scarce, they were rated as even better. There is a powerful assumption that things that become scarce before our eyes are more valuable.

The final revelation was the importance of the reason that Worchel and his colleagues gave for why some cookies were taken away. Some participants were told simply that a mistake had been made. Others were told that the cookies were needed for another person. The people who were told that the cookies were needed to give to someone else gave them the highest quality rating in the whole experiment. The assumption is that if someone else wants something, they must value it, so we should too.

Worchel's experiment and others indicate that these responses to scarcity are almost universally embedded in our unconscious programming. It is an automatic human reaction to want what we can't have. These responses are easily triggered at the end of a relationship. We automatically want something that has recently become scarce, unavailable or given to someone else. That is why, even if you decided to end the relationship, you could experience feelings of desiring your ex once more, simply and precisely because he or she is no longer available. If your ex is going out with someone else, that fact alone can cause a totally automatic response of wanting them again, just like the cookies that were taken away to be given to someone else.

Often when we do things automatically, we do not notice we are doing them. The key to stopping the scarcity principle from driving your behavior is to become aware of it. As we saw earlier, your conscious awareness includes the ability to make choices. As soon as you become aware of an automatic response you bring to it the possibility of questioning the trigger and changing the response. That is why bringing conscious awareness to unconscious behavior reduces its power. Now that you know about the scarcity principle, you can see that if you had a longing for your ex, it is not necessarily deeply personal. It could simply be an automatic response.

"HE HAD AN AFFAIR, HE BROKE MY HEART, BUT NOW HE WON'T LEAVE ME ALONE"

The attractiveness of scarcity accounts for many cases of exes trying to get back together. But one woman who came to see me illustrated a very different reason why exes try to start up again. Lori didn't know how to deal with her ex. He had had an affair and she'd thrown him out, but then he begged her to forgive him and take him back. Eventually she relented and they got together again. Then he did it again, so she finished with him completely. She came to see me, because he was still calling her all the time and she didn't know how to get rid of him. She had been very fond of him, but she knew she couldn't trust him. She also couldn't understand him. If he loved her enough to pursue her so hard, how come he went and had another affair?

From what she told me about her ex, Bob, I guessed that underneath his successful, driven exterior he might suffer from low self-esteem. I asked Lori to imagine putting herself in his shoes, and imagine that underneath the facade he felt bad about himself.

Bob meets a beautiful woman who falls in love with him. Suddenly he has got all he ever wanted on a plate. Lori is tall and blonde, good-looking and intelligent. She is the woman of his dreams. But deep down he doesn't believe he deserves her. Bob thinks he is a fraud. He is not as confident as he pretends to be, he worries that he is not as good-looking as he would like to be, and he is not sure that he can live up to what he imagines Lori will ask of him. The longer he is with her, the closer he feels her to be—and the closer she wants to get. The closer she gets, the more frightened he is that she will discover the "real" Bob—the fraud.

He gets scared and he wants someone to comfort him, but he dare not turn to Lori, because he thinks she will leave when he tells her of his fears. He meets a younger woman at a party who makes it clear she fancies him. It is possible, it's easy, it's flattering to his ego, so he goes to bed with her. The conquest boosts his self-esteem. But Bob doesn't take his lover seriously, so he doesn't feel he needs to open up to her. He can still play the cool, successful man about town. Then Lori finds out and gives him the boot.

Bob's world falls to pieces. The woman of his dreams has walked out of his life. He is desperate. He begs her to take him back. He tells her she is wonderful and that he needs her and there is no one else in his world who could ever mean as much to him as she does. Bob will say anything and do anything to get her back except tell the truth: that he feels unworthy of her love. He won't tell her that because he doesn't want to admit it to himself, and even if he did, he is sure that if he tells her it will put her off forever.

By sheer persistence Bob got Lori back the first time. And they went back to square one. He is still frightened to open up to her completely, and now he has the added stress of trying to prove that he wouldn't even look at another woman. Eventually the stress builds up, and he finds relief from his troubles when a charming younger woman flirts with him at a party. And the cycle begins again.

Bob and Lori both forgot that nobody is perfect. Bob tried to pretend he was better than he feared he was, and ended up behaving worse than he needed to. Lori fell for Bob's act, and then was hurt when he cheated on her. Lori needed to remember that if someone pretends they are not vulnerable or that their life is perfect, they are lying.

It is common in the early stages of a relationship to

play up your strengths or pretend to be a little better than you are, but part of getting closer is admitting your own bullshit, and teasing your partner about theirs. There is no need to get stuck pretending to be someone you are not, or to believe anyone is 100 percent wonderful in every aspect of their life.

"HE REFUSES TO ADMIT IT IS ALL OVER"

Francesca came to see me three days after she had told her boyfriend, Terry, that it was all over. Their relationship first got into trouble when she found out he was taking a lot of drugs. When she confronted him he tried to persuade her that it was no big deal. But Francesca insisted he give up or they split up. Eventually he agreed to stop.

Francesca really enjoyed being with Terry, and she found herself imagining the wedding. She would daydream about the dress, the church and her father standing up and giving a speech—the whole deal.

Terry was very busy at work, so she had plenty of time to dream. Once or twice he stood her up or forgot to phone and she felt a twinge of suspicion that he was taking drugs, but she didn't want to nag him, so she kept quiet. And so they carried on. He was working harder and harder and she carried on dreaming about the wedding. Then one day she came home unexpectedly and found him with a pile of cocaine.

He said it was a one-time thing and promised to

stop immediately. He even flushed it down the toilet in front of her eyes. She forgave him, and Terry made more of an effort to be around for her. She still felt suspicious but she decided that positive thinking was the way forward. Then one night he acted so strangely that she was convinced he'd been using. He flatly denied it but the following day he admitted it, again claiming it was a one-time thing. Soon there was another "one-time thing." Then another, and another.

Terry was completely addicted, and she couldn't get him to stop. She fought with him, she screamed, she pleaded. They split up and they got back together again and again. One day, in desperation or frustration, or simply because she had tried everything else, Francesca took some cocaine with Terry. Then she did it again. One day, a few weeks later, Francesca woke up and found herself half undressed on the floor next to an empty vodka bottle, and realized she was living in a nightmare. All the dreadful incidents of the relationship crowded into her mind at once and she said to herself, "That's it. It's over."

Francesca had crossed her threshold. It was the last straw. Just like the women who had been beaten up by their husbands one time too many, she woke up and saw that the whole relationship was a con. Terry wasn't able to love her properly because he couldn't even run his own life.

Francesca knew she had to get out of the relationship for her own safety. She told Terry she wouldn't see him anymore. She still loved him, but she saw that his life was out of control, and she didn't dare to be with him. She was scared to be with him. But Terry kept trying. He wouldn't take no for an answer. He kept asking to meet her just one more time. He would call her after a drug binge and say he needed her and that without her he would kill himself. He used every argument he could think of. He refused to hear her saying no.

As Francesca told me her story she realized that she had denied a lot of her own feelings. She had compulsively tried to keep the relationship going, even when Terry was behaving badly. She kept finding excuses for his behavior. Francesca began to see that she had been as desperate for the relationship to work as Terry had been desperate about his drugs.

We began to look at why she was so desperate. Deep down Francesca felt she was lucky to have Terry. Although she was a strikingly attractive woman, she didn't really have the confidence she appeared to have. She felt bad about herself and invested all her energy in keeping the relationship going rather than dealing with her own feelings.

Francesca and Terry's relationship was built on denial. The more she dreamed, the less she noticed the warning signs in Terry's behavior. When he insisted he was clean, she ignored the feeling she had that he was lying. But her feelings were trying to help her.

I asked Francesca to look back over her relationship and write down what had really happened and how she would have felt if she hadn't been lost in dreaming about paradise.

Francesca was writing out her new viewpoint on her relationship when Terry rang. This time she didn't deny her feelings. She was very, very angry. She told him, in detail, just how much he had hurt her. She told him how painful it had been to put so much into helping him and believing in him and then to be betrayed. When she spoke her truth, Terry finally heard her say no. Terry still tried for some time to get her to take him back, but that conversation was the turning point. Francesca wasn't lying any more. **If you lie, then non-verbally you invite others to lie to you. When you speak your truth, it calls to the truth in the other person.**

Francesca's story illustrates another point. Very often the problems we have when a relationship ends are the same as the problems that occurred within the relationship. Francesca and Terry were both in denial in their own ways during the relationship. When they split up, Terry tried to deny the split was real, and Francesca tried to deny how hurt she was. When Francesca gave up her denial, she found herself free of the relationship and free of her longing for Terry.

BLAME

Another enemy of change is blame. We can't move on until we stop blaming, just as we can't make real changes until we give up denial. Blame is a way of saying, "You are making me have my painful feelings." Actually, short of physically torturing them, no one can make another person feel bad. One person's feelings cannot be controlled by another person. It is your subjective response to what you hear or experience that makes your feelings. Whenever we blame people for our feelings we are denying our own power to change our feelings. Even if blaming seems to be justified, it won't help you.

The position that the blamer wants to claim is that of victim. If my troubles are *your* fault, I don't have to take responsibility for them. A perfect illustration of how devastating blame can be is the case of Vince, who had separated from his wife, Linda, after they had been married for ten years. They'd had their ups and downs and one of the downs was that the spice had gone out of their sex life. One evening Linda found Vince looking at naked women on the Internet. He suggested to her that they should try a threesome. She told him she wasn't interested.

A month or so later she told him she wanted to separate. She said his suggestion of a threesome had undermined her sexual confidence.

Vince went into shock. He just stood there while Linda recited a long catalogue of all the things she said he had done to hurt and abuse her, culminating in looking at porn on the Internet and suggesting a threesome, and then she walked out the door.

Vince called me in tears. From the moment she left he had been going over and over the things she accused him of and feeling stupid, guilty and wretched about all of them. When he managed to tell me the whole story of what happened when Linda left, I saw that the words she had spoken had hit him like a hypnotic suggestion.

When she told him she was leaving, he went into shock. In shock, his critical faculties were stunned. Everything she said was absorbed without question. This pattern is very common in the trauma of a breakup. The shock inhibits the normal ability to question and evaluate accusations. As a result, unchallenged blaming statements start running on autopilot. Linda's words were going round and round in Vince's head, and all he could think about were the bad things she said he had done. Vince needed to reengage his ability to challenge her words.

I asked him to go back in his memory to the evening when he had suggested the threesome and imagine watching a videotape of the whole scene. I asked him to see himself in the video and to see Linda and to think about what each of them said. I asked him to pay particular attention also to what each of them did.

Then I asked him to do the same thing with the evening when she had walked out. I asked him to tell me what he thought had gone on. Seeing the scene from the outside allowed Vince to think about it differently. Because he wasn't stunned by the shock, he could analyze and criticize what had happened from a neutral position.

The first thing he saw about the evening when he suggested the threesome was that Linda had not acted hugely upset. Nor had she acted differently or strangely from that moment. In other words, his suggestion did not seem to cause a massive change in her. Next he remembered that neither of them had discussed it since that evening. Then he saw that Linda had not tried to talk to him on the evening she left—she had just delivered her speech and gone. Imagining seeing the scene from the outside broke the power of the hypnotic suggestion in Linda's words, and Vince could see that the situation was not exactly as she had described it. It later turned out that Linda had been having an affair for several months and had used Vince's suggestion as an opportunity to make him into the bad guy.

VICTIMS, PERSECUTORS AND RESCUERS

As we discussed it further, it became clear that Linda had cast herself as the victim and was treating Vince like a persecutor. She was blaming him for making her feel bad sexually. She called up all their friends and blamed the whole thing on him.

When he realized what was going on, Vince felt that *he* was the victim, because of the way Linda treated him and then gossiped to their friends. He thought she was being self-righteous and blaming everything on him although she had not made any real effort to sort out their problems herself.

When Vince told me that he felt like the real victim I pointed out that the two of them were swapping roles: Victim and Persecutor. When one of them took one role, the other person took the other role. And the pair of them left the door open for a third role-player: the Rescuer. For Linda, her lover was playing that role.

Victim and Persecutor is a dangerous game. If one person blames the other for all their problems, the person being blamed is likely to do the same. Eventually one or both will go and find someone or something else to rescue them. It may be an affair, or it may be drink, drugs or some other distraction. But the rescue will only be temporary. The real way out is to understand that, however bad or difficult your partner was, no single person is ever to blame for all the problems in a relationship. You contributed too, even if only by going along with it.

Linda contributed to the decline of her marriage by having an affair, by not discussing her dissatisfaction with their sex life and by not telling Vince sooner how upset she was by the things she later accused him of. Vince contributed by failing to tell her how much he loved her and failing to try other ways to talk about their sex life.

In the final analysis the root of their problems was not his suggestion, nor even her affair, but the fact that they did not communicate adequately about their difficulties. Whether they got back together or not, each of them had to give up the role of Victim or Persecutor, and take on the responsibility of doing their own rescuing for themselves.

Watch the Movie

Do you feel bad because of what your ex has told
you? Do you think that you are to blame for everything? It can be very instructive to use the video
technique to review what happened and see
whether what people did corresponds with
what they said. What people do and what they
say are not always the same thing. And sometimes people ask others to obey rules they do
not stick to themselves.

1. Imagine you have a movie of your relationship
   and that you are watching it on a screen that
   only shows black-and-white pictures. Rewind
   it to the events that your ex says are your fault
   and are the reason why it all went wrong.

2. Replay the video, making sure you imagine yourself outside the scene, watching, comfortably separate from the feelings of the people inside it.

3. Watch carefully and notice if anything seems or looks different from this perspective.

4. Stop after each accusation and ask yourself what your ex would have to say if they took responsibility for their own role in the situation.

5. Now do the whole thing again, with the sound turned down whenever your ex is speaking. Pay close attention to what they do, not what they say. Generally speaking what people do is a hundred times more important than what they say.

OVERCOMING JEALOUSY AND
OBSESSIVE THOUGHTS

Vince felt much better when he had reviewed his imaginary video of what had happened. But he was also bothered by the fact that Linda had a lover. He felt jealous.

Jealousy causes so much pain and difficulty you might think it deserved a whole chapter to itself. But it doesn't. Although jealousy can be truly horrible and vile, the way it is created is incredibly simple. It is so simple to create, and so simple to dismantle, that we are going to fit it all into less than two pages.

To help Vince stop feeling jealous I showed him one of the simplest yet most powerful techniques I know. It's called "white it out." This is why it works. Jealousy is a three-stage process. If anyone is going to feel jealous, they have to go through these three stages. First, they have to make a picture of something they want that they haven't got. Second, they have to see someone else having it. Third, they have to say to themselves, "That person has it, I want it and I can't have it."

If you are not doing step one, you can't get to step two, and you won't get to step three. If you are not imagining what you haven't got, you can't be jealous. This technique simply eliminates stage one. If you use white it out whenever you get to stage one, you don't get jealous.

I spoke to Vince a week after I taught him this technique. He told me he had practiced it fifty times a day. He hadn't phoned Linda at all, and in fact she had phoned just before we spoke. "You know, the funny thing is," he said, "I'm not sure I can remember exactly what she looks like."

I spoke to Vince again, about a month later, and he said that he did miss Linda, and he did feel grief about it from time to time, but he wasn't guilt-tripping anymore and he was getting on with his life. And he said he had realized that a few things about his own behavior needed changing and he was going to do a little work on himself for a while before he got involved again with someone else.

White It Out

Eliminate jealousy and obsessive thoughts with this simple technique. On some video cameras there is a button to control the amount of light being let in. If you turn it up all the way, the picture disappears because there is so much light that it is "whited out."

1. Whenever a picture that makes you jealous comes into your mind immediately turn the brightness up and up and up until it whites out.

2. Do this whenever any scene that makes you jealous or any image of your ex occurs in your head and you will soon make whiting out an automatic process.

3. If you repeat this process over and over again, it automates to the point where it is almost impossible to think of the image anymore.

DON'T GET MAD, DON'T GET EVEN— GET OUT

Trying to settle the score or being angry with your ex is continuing the relationship but with negative instead of positive feelings. A simple way to stop negative feelings taking up your time is to go out and meet new people who start new relationships and new stories in your life.

People who hide themselves away with their pain tend to mope. The more that mopers mope, the less they feel like going out. So they do a bit more moping and feel even less inclined to go out. One problem, heartbreak, becomes two problems—heartbreak and isolation.

People who socialize recover more quickly from a breakup. The more they socialize, the more people they meet and the more they see that the world still turns with all its joys and tragedies. They see other people have their trials and triumphs, too. One problem that in isolation felt huge becomes smaller when it shares the stage with other stories of struggles and success.

So get out there. You don't have to date, you don't have to flirt, you don't have to hang around in bars, you don't have to talk about your ex, or your situation, or anything else in particular. You don't have to be the life and soul of the party; you only have to be polite. Just go out and mix with people.

Socializing is not a miracle cure all on its own, but it always helps people to feel better faster, and to remember that their own troubles are just part of what is going on in the big, wide world. If you do meet someone else who is interesting that's fine, but it is not the point of the exercise and it certainly isn't necessary. Just go out with your old friends or make some new ones. Go out and talk to people and do things. That's all. Just do it.

"My ex is trying to turn our friends against me"

Being with friends is one of the easiest and most important ways to feel better. Friends don't have to do anything special, they don't have to have any special skills, you don't have to talk about anything in particular. You don't have to talk about how you feel if you don't want to. It is just good to be reminded that there are other people you are fond of. And being with friends who love you is good for you. Indeed, especially when you are not sure you feel like it, it is worth making an effort to see your friends.

Some of your friends are likely also to be friends of your ex. They might want to see you but feel a little awkward. It is very important not to ask them to take sides. Let them choose and let them take their own time to do it. They might have all sorts of other loyalties and agendas to deal with. Usually all it takes is a little time for people to get used to the new situation. And if a friend does not call for a while, you may think they don't care, but try not to make your judgments out loud. You never know the whole story of someone else's situation. They might simply need more time to sort things out. If they really are no friend of yours then it doesn't matter what they think or who they are. In that case, they are just someone in your past.

If your ex tries to set some of your friends against you, don't get drawn into a battle. Just make it clear to your friends that you value each of them for who they are, and that you want to see them. What they do with the rest of their time is their business. In the end everyone will end up in the company they feel most at ease in, so there is little point in trying to force people to make a choice.

LAUGH

Yes, laugh. Don't take it so seriously. When we laugh we trigger positive feelings because, as we saw in chapter 1, the body affects the mind just as much as the mind affects the body. Smiling and laughing make us happy, just as happiness makes us smile and laugh.

Laughter—even forced laughter—makes us smile. And even forced smiles have a positive effect. Remember: We are not trying to mask or evade our emotions; we are just adding a few moments of light relief to life. We are stimulating our natural ability to feel good in ourselves. We do have to face and deal with some difficult emotions—but we can't do it all the time. When we are not actually processing difficult feelings we don't have to keep them going. So you might as well feel good. Try it. Laugh at something, anything, even the idea of yourself trying to laugh, for five minutes a day.

Return to Sender

However hard you try, there will be times when you have to see your ex, or you bump into them by accident. It can be annoying, even depressing, if you felt fine before you saw them and then you find you are left with a bad feeling afterwards. I have a great little technique for situations like this. I call it "return to sender."

I created this technique when I was studying family systems theory and I saw that families dish out emotional jobs the way they dish out household jobs. Just as someone might do the shopping and someone else might do the washing-up, so too does one person usually do the encouraging, another the nurturing, and so on. What is interesting is that if the nurturer, say, is absent, another one takes over the role. It reminded me of the children's party game called pass the parcel.

Then I realized what had been happening to some of my clients. They had been given a parcel of feelings or jobs that didn't belong to them. If you are feeling fine and you meet someone and twenty minutes later they leave and you feel bad, it is reasonable to assume that your bad feeling came from them. So, if it belongs to them, you should send it back.

The technique is very simple. Even though it may seem almost like a game, when you do this you will see that visual imagination has a powerful effect on feelings.

1. Notice where you feel the bad feeling in your body.

2. Imagine a shape and a color for it.

3. Then imagine moving it out, as though putting it on a table in front of you.

4. Imagine wrapping it up like a parcel.

5. Then imagine throwing it away from you with such force that it goes over the horizon all the way to your ex.

6. Now notice how you feel.

7. If there are any leftover bits of feeling lying around, do the same again until you feel as comfortable as you like.

5

WHY DID IT HAPPEN TO ME, AND HOW CAN I STOP IT FROM HAPPENING AGAIN?

Do you ever wonder why it happened? Why did you pick the man or woman who would break your heart? Why did you have to pick that person and not someone else? Why not someone more suitable, someone who wanted to stay? And why did they pick you?

Maybe you were unlucky. Maybe it was just an accident. And maybe not. We are not always aware of the forces that are influencing us. We live amid a multitude of them: social, cultural, biological and unconscious. All of them play upon us all the time. The main forces that influence why people get together fall into three categories:

- Choice
- Context
- Imprinting

CHOICE

Deliberate choice is the factor to which we pay most attention. Do I want him or don't I? Which one do I prefer? Should I flirt or not? How far should I go? Do I dare ask her out? People talk for hours about who they'd like to go out with, what their chances are, what they'll do to get them. They spend ages agonizing over what to do and then summoning up the courage to do it.

Ironically, our own conscious choice is usually the least influential factor in determining the relationship we end up in. This is just as true when we start a deliberate campaign of seduction as it is when we find ourselves in a relationship we had no intention of starting. The factors that cause us to fancy someone enough to pursue them are beyond our conscious control. We might choose how to try to win someone, but choice cannot strike that spark that makes us want the relationship in the first place.

Context

Context affects our relationships in the simplest way possible. We always pick our partners from among the people we meet. You can't go out with someone you haven't met. Even if you meet at a distance via the Internet, the Internet itself provides the context. You are both people who are open to relationships that arise from surfing the Net.

This may appear so obvious that you wonder why I bother saying it, but it is worth realizing how much our context is determined by our choices and those of the people around us. Each of us comes from a certain type of family with certain expectations. As we conform to them, or rebel against them, we find ourselves in particular groups.

If you are a churchgoer, you meet other churchgoers. If you are a clubber, you meet other clubbers. Contexts are created by habits, too. If you are a smoker, you are likely to meet other smokers. People who stop smoking change their context, and in due course find they make more nonsmoking friends.

Where you live is a more obvious example of the effect of context. In a cosmopolitan city like London or New York or Paris or Berlin, you could meet someone from almost any background imaginable. In a quiet rural town there is less variety.

As well as social, behavioral and geographical contexts, cultural contexts also affect us. Ideas of love, conventions of courtship and norms of number and type of sexual partner are just as powerful in modern society as they are in any distant society studied by an anthropologist. Most of us are more likely than not to end up with someone of the same religion, with the same sort of background and the same sort of financial situation. If you don't want that to happen, you might have to make a special effort to move into another context.

IMPRINTING

Easily the biggest influence on our choice of partner is the imprinting we receive from our families. The traces our families leave on us are profound and yet so subtle that it is possible to remain unconscious of them one's entire life. And yet they are continually at work, and above all they are at work in the choices we make of the people we work with, play with and marry.

There is a fascinating exercise used in the training of family therapists that reveals just how sophisticated is the unconscious mechanism by which people choose each other. Very early on, before they've had a chance to get to know each other, the trainees are gathered together in a large room and asked to walk around and pick out a partner who seems to fit with their family in some way. When they have arranged themselves in couples, each couple is asked to find another couple with whom they seem to fit. The crucial instruction of the exercise is that the whole thing must be done without any talking. The trainees walk round in silence and pair up in silence. Then the pairs pair up in silence.

Then, at last, they are allowed to talk. They are asked to talk to the members of their group about their families. Invariably the participants find that they have picked out three other trainees with whom they share significant similarities in family backgrounds. How do they do it?

Whenever we meet someone we form a sense of who they are. We read each other's expression, posture, walk and a thousand other signals quite automatically. All our gestures, mannerisms and expressions are non-verbal signals that reflect our emotional habits.

A simple illustration of a basic level at which this works is that if someone is usually cheerful they smile a lot so their face gradually acquires the creases of smile lines. Over time their face will tend to settle in a cheery expression which we all recognize. As we saw earlier, the basic emotions and their expressions are human constants and are universally understood, regardless of culture.

But the creation and reading of signals is also a more subtle process. As we saw in chapter 1, everything in the conscious and unconscious mind is reflected in the body. Our patterns of thought and feeling gradually influence every cell of the body. There are patterns of movement and posture associated with certain characteristics of which we have no inkling at a conscious level, but which we recognize and react to at an unconscious level.

As we spend all our lives immersed in the human soup of society we cannot help but learn to make more and more sense of what we see in the people around us. We hardly ever put into words the amount we understand one another, but we have a specific response to everyone we meet. We do it so casually and so unconsciously that we don't pay much attention to it. If we meet a great many people at once we have so little time to pay conscious attention that our reactions are modulated at a completely unconscious level.

FAMILY

But certain people stand out to us. These are people who have emotional patterns that are extremely familiar to us. They are family—because they are like our own family. We are able to pick them out from a crowd of strangers. If you meet someone who looks or sounds pleasant to you and whose emotional patterns are familiar to you, you are likely to feel closer to them than to people whose families were very different.

Each and every one of us unthinkingly learns a huge array of feelings, behaviors and beliefs from our family. All of these dynamics play on our features, actions and bodies, and as time passes they leave their traces in everything from our speech patterns to our posture.

From our family's actions we deduce how men should treat women, and how women should treat men. We learn how to socialize, how to behave in public and in private, how to respond to our own impulses and how to deal with the demands of others. And from the way our families treat us, we make deductions about our own self-worth, the value of our own responses, what we can expect from life and how to get our needs met. Our beliefs about what love is, what it means and how to show it all come from our families.

Even though we learn quickly that other people's lives are different, nearly all of us continue to behave as though the emotional dynamics of our family of origin were the basic structure underlying all emotional behavior. In a sense we learn from our families how to be people.

Our family is the source of our first definition of normality. To children the attitudes and behavior of their parents seem "normal" because they have no means of comparison. Inevitably, each family creates different patterns and expectations, which family members feel are normal. These differing expectations and notions of normality are a common source of friction in relationships. Whereas differences are relatively easy to work out when they are obvious, they are more problematic when they are hidden by the fact that we use the same words to describe different things.

When we grow up and leave the family home we rapidly expand our repertoire of behavior. We meet different people in different circumstances and many of us consciously and deliberately choose different attitudes and lifestyles from those of our parents. As a result most of us feel that we have long left our family ways behind us by the time we get into serious relationships. But although we have expanded our repertoire of relational dynamics, we have not rewritten it. Our family of origin still furnishes the template for our most intimate relationships.

Unmet needs

A widespread theory of psychotherapy has it that in a relationship each of us is trying to get from our partners what we didn't get from our parents. As the jargon has it, we are trying to get our partners to "meet our unmet needs." There is plenty of evidence to support this. For example, if your mother and father encouraged and trusted you, the chances are that you grew up to have confidence in yourself. A child whose parents were hypercritical and never gave praise, on the other hand, would probably never be sure that its actions, or even its being, was adequate, and could well grow up to lack confidence. Such a child would feel insecure and find it difficult to trust their own judgment. The child would tend to look to others for reassurance. So, in due course, as an adult he or she would turn to their partner for the reassurance they didn't get from their parents.

However, although there is plenty of evidence to support this view, it does not offer a complete explanation. I have met many unconfident clients whose parents apparently were very encouraging, and equally there are plenty of people who did not get much praise or trust who have grown up to be confident and successful.

It is also clear that the needs of a child are not identical to the needs of an adult in a romantic relationship. This theory seems tantalizingly close to the truth, and yet it does not explain enough about adult-to-adult relationships.

Parents as role models

Another traditional view holds that our parents are the most important people in our early lives. Your father is the first man in your life, so he becomes the model for all men, and your mother is the first woman in your life, so she becomes the model for all women. In other words, Dad is the ideal man and Mom is the ideal woman. We must remember that the claim is that this is an unconscious drive. Many of us quite deliberately try to get away from our parents and their way of doing things, but the theory is that, despite this, as we grew up we got programmed to look for a partner who was as like our opposite sex parent as possible.

There does seem to be some evidence that this occurs sometimes, but it does not seem to be quite enough. There are also myriad counterexamples. If the theory was true, then brothers would find themselves very similar women to marry and sisters would marry similar men. You only have to look around a few families to see that is far from universally the case.

A variation on this theory states that as adults we treat female partners as if they were like our mothers or male partners as if they were like our fathers. We project onto our partners the expectation that they will treat us in the same way that our father or mother treated us. Again there is evidence for this view. After all, a common enough remark in a relationship is "Stop treating me like your mother!" But if we do treat our partners like a parent, couldn't it be that a part of us has not grown up yet?

That certainly would seem a simpler explanation. The crucial question is which partners do we pick and how do we relate to them when we are independent and adult enough not to fall into a parent-child dynamic?

Furthermore, many clients have told me, "But my dad wasn't there. My mom brought me up on her own. How can my dad influence me if he wasn't there?" Research has shown that absent parents do have an effect. The child sees one parent coping on their own and that becomes a powerful model. At the same time, in the absence of the other real parent, the child projects into the void a highly idealistic fantasy of who they are. As the child doesn't see the absent parent very much, or at all, these projections are not tempered by much reality.

The upshot is that people who are most likely to become single parents are people who were brought up by single parents. It seems that every parent role does have an effect.

I had a client whose father was an alcoholic. Her mother was the only source of stability and regular income in the family. My client grew up to be a very successful businesswoman. As a young woman she swore she would never end up with someone like her father. She didn't. In fact, she became a single parent. It was only years later in therapy that she saw that she had had highly unrealistic expectations of her son's father, and had ended up with very little support from him, just as her mother had had very little support from her father.

Couple imprinting

The theories of role models, unmet needs and projections of our parents explain some things and yet also give rise to complications. There are many cases that don't fit the theories, and the mechanism by which they work or influence us becomes more obscure the closer you look at it. None of these theories really convinced me.

Then I discovered that what is imprinted on us is our parents' relationship. **Their behavior towards each other is the blueprint for how we set out to make our own relationships.** In respect of how we conduct our couple relationships, **how our parents treated each other is more significant than how they treated us.**

I owe this insight to a remarkable Gestalt therapist in New Orleans called Anne Teachworth. Anne has been doing couple counseling for more than twenty years. She learned all the traditional theories in her training, and like the rest of us found that they did explain a fair amount of what happened to her clients a fair amount of the time. But they didn't explain enough. And that bothered her. Anne realized that what is significant is that throughout your childhood you witness the relationship between your parents. It is as though you are watching a training video in couple relationships. In other words, everything your mother and father do tells you, "This is how couples relate to each other." It is the parental relationship, not the opposite sex parent, that is the key determinant in our unconscious programming.

Anne discovered that when we grow up and begin to have our own relationships, we have an unconscious drive to replicate the parental relationship because that, at an unconscious level, is what we expect a relationship to be. Even if we consciously hated how our parents behaved, the expectation at an unconscious level is so strong that without being aware of it we seek out a partner who will assist us to reproduce their patterns.

We do this by choosing one of the roles in our parents' relationship. The role we choose for ourselves is the role of the parent whom we preferred, regardless of sex. A little girl who preferred her father would take on his way of behaving in a couple relationship, not her mother's. You would take on the role of the same-sex parent if they were also the parent whose behavior you liked most.

Having chosen one role, the unconscious is then on the lookout for someone to fill the other role. It is not looking for someone who looks or sounds like the other parent, nor someone with the same interests or accent or any other external attribute. The single, highly motivating attractor is the emotional behavior patterns. In almost every case we are unaware of this. We think we have chosen our partner because they are handsome or pretty, intelligent or witty, or just because they charmed us. Those reasons may all be true, but the unconscious preselected them as an option because their deep emotional patterns fitted the role it was seeking. The first we know of it is when we find ourselves attracted to someone, or find a relationship "takes us over."

Sometimes, however, and often after a number of relationships have not worked out, we become so annoyed with our own behavior and the people we have picked that we make a conscious, determined decision to change entirely. We refuse to contemplate a partner who was anything like our last one.

That sounds like a good move. And sometimes it is. But, unhappily, the most common outcome is simply that we move from behaving like our favorite parent to behaving like the other one. The unconscious seeks out a mate who behaves as we used to. We have just swapped roles. Have you ever found yourself treating a partner just how an ex used to treat you? It can be a nasty surprise. Now you know why it happens.

Family hypnosis

Another question occurs to most of my clients sooner or later. Although this theory rings true, and they are able to trace its effect in their lives, the question arises, "Even if my parents were like that, how did it have such a profound effect on me?" And furthermore, "Why is it in my unconscious? Why have I not been aware of it? If it was that powerful, that influential and that important, wouldn't it be right at the front of my mind?"

Most of us leave home to strike out on our own and reject some if not all of our parents' ideas. We are exposed to all sorts of other people and hundreds of other relationships. Surely that will also have an effect? Why should childhood experiences be more influential and be imprinted in the unconscious?

It is true that our adult experience does have an effect on us, but that effect is primarily on our conscious mind. We make our conscious decisions in the light of our understanding of our experiences. But to see why our childhood family experience is so powerful, we need to look at the special conditions of our early existence.

When you are born, your family and the home you are in is your entire world. You don't know anything beyond it. Everything you see and feel around you is simply the way things are because you have nothing else to compare it with. So your parents' relationship is how moms and dads relate. There is no other example. Your first impressions of relationships in your childhood define them before you even think of questioning them.

Your parents' relationship was like an atmosphere in which you lived as a child. You were so used to it that it was invisible, like water is invisible to a fish, and air is invisible to us. But you picked up and responded to every element of that atmosphere, just as you feel and react to the wind and the temperature of the air around you. It was so natural you didn't question it, and yet you absorbed its influence all the time.

Your conscious mind hardly ever thought about your parents' relationship. Fish don't think about water, and we hardly ever think about the air we breathe, or the fact that we are breathing it every second of our lives. We take it for granted, just as you took your family for granted.

In three ways this immersion in the family is similar to experiences in hypnosis. In the first place, in hypnotic trance you focus on one thing at a time and this leads to a state of fascination or absorption, where what you are aware of becomes the whole of your world. You don't make comparisons; you just accept that what is around you is as it appears. The absorption of trance makes the subject accept his or her environment as the only reality. This is similar to the child's attitude to the family.

Secondly, your critical faculties are suspended in trance. Hypnosis induces a sort of literalism, where things are taken at face value. You don't analyze things or question them. That's why when I tell people at my shows that they are riding horses they don't ask me, "Oh, where did the horses come from?" They just immediately treat their chairs as though they were horses. As young children, our critical facilities have not yet developed, so we cannot question family behavior any more than hypnotic subjects can question the hypnotist.

Thirdly, in trance everything happens automatically. In fact, we go in and out of trance all day when we do things on automatic. Families have habits and routines that family members carry out without thinking. We take them for granted and act them out without having to think about them. It is the same in hypnotic trance. In hypnosis we let the unconscious mind run things, so from the point of view of the conscious mind they happen all by themselves: on automatic. A splendid example of this is one of the oldest and most intriguing demonstrations of hypnosis: arm levitation. The hypnotist makes

suggestions to the unconscious mind that cause the hypnotic subject's arm to rise all by itself. The subject is
making no effort, nor having any conscious intention to
make the arm lift, and yet it becomes weightless and they
see it going up in front of their eyes. The entire movement is autonomous.

Every family has hundreds of routines that work just
like hypnosis. You can see a good example of this if you
have a friend or partner you know well whom you met
independently of their family circle. If you go with that
person when they visit their family you will see them behave in all sorts of ways you have never seen before. As
an adult each of us chooses how to behave, but when we
visit our family their familiar faces, voices and actions
work like posthypnotic suggestions to trigger behavioral
patterns that were embedded in us in our childhood.

That's also why you can go to visit your parents feeling grounded, grown-up and amicable, and find yourself
half an hour later in exactly the sort of shouting match
you had as a teenager. It takes a particular effort to avoid
falling into the family trance and to stop rerunning old
arguments with our parents.

REPLICATING RELATIONSHIPS

We understand couple relationships primarily in
terms of our parents' relationship, so that is the
understanding we take into the future with us. To be in a
relationship means, at an unconscious level, to behave

like that. The total outcome of the family imprinting and the hypnotic situation in which it occurs is to bury expectations about couples in your unconscious mind where they are not available for critical analysis or inspection. However, these expectations constantly guide our emotions and affections by making us believe that people who behave towards us as our parents behaved towards each other are naturally compelling and attractive.

We did not witness our parents courting or getting together, so the manner in which we do that is all our own, although it is driven by the unconscious recognition of our intended's relationship potential. However, as soon as we behave or think of ourselves as a couple the expectations and behavioral patterns spring into action.

That's why people can change so much between the flirting, chasing and courting stage and the couple stage of a relationship. So many times you hear people complain, "He wasn't like that before I married him."

If your parents had relationship troubles, you might be vulnerable to similar ones. And most of our parents—who aren't perfect any more than anyone else is—had their troubles. A big difference recently, however, has been the rise in divorces and one-parent families. Surely Anne's theory would predict that each generation would end up like the one before. How come more people split up now?

The answer is, simply, because we can. We have fewer children than our parents did and on average we have them later. Women have more and more financial independence; the state provides more assistance for single parents and it is easier to find housing for singles and single parents than it was a few decades ago when there was social pressure to get married and stay married. The social pressure to conform to relationship norms has radically reduced.

So we split because we are able to. In the past it is likely that for every couple who stayed together because they wanted to, there was another who stayed together because they had to. Some of them, of course, got through their troubles and learned to love each other more deeply. Others learned to live separate emotional lives together in the same home. None of us is in a position to judge these relationships, because we don't know the inside story.

However, most of us nowadays do not want to carry on in a continuous cycle of having one relationship after another and splitting up again and again. We are now in a position to change the unconscious patterns we bring to relationships.

THE SOLUTION

If you keep finding the same sort of person and ending up having the same sort of problems, you need to change. You didn't choose all that trouble. It came your way because of the patterns imprinted in your unconscious. We can't erase those patterns but we can install new, more healthy ones. When you mentally rehearse new patterns you will build up the corresponding neural pathways. It is a bit like diverting a river. You don't try to fill in the old riverbed, you just divert the water to your new route so that it carves a new riverbed. Eventually the new riverbed will be deeper than the old one and your diversion will become the permanent course of the river. Like diverting the river, mental rehearsal is teaching your unconscious through repetition to follow the new path rather than the old one.

I had a client whose father had been downright vicious to her mother. He had affairs under her nose. He put her down all the time in private and ignored her in public. They argued all the time. He never paid much attention to my client, his daughter, either. He didn't go out of his way to encourage or praise her. Instead he called on her for help when he was feeling down. She spent her childhood worrying about him because he told her his problems and never seemed to have any solutions. When she was seventeen, an older man fell passionately in love with her and she ran off with him in defiance of her parents' wishes. It was only looking back on it some years later that my client realized that he too was a charming depressive, like her father. Later on she kept finding to her chagrin that the men she had relationships with were depressive or unfaithful, like her father.

I asked this client to do the reimprinting exercise that follows. She leant back in the chair in my study, closed her eyes and then five seconds later opened them and said, "I'm sorry. I can't do this. It is just impossible. My father would never have told my mother she was right. And he just wasn't affectionate. I never saw him kiss her."

I reminded her that she was not meant to believe in these imaginary scenes, simply to see them as vividly as possible. She tried again and managed it, but when she opened her eyes she reported that it made her feel extremely weird. "Exactly," I said. "That is why this is so powerful and so important. If it was of no consequence it wouldn't have any effect. The fact that it makes you feel extremely weird even to imagine your father being affectionate shows how profoundly you are affected. When you can do this and feel comfortable, happy and relaxed, the changes in your unconscious behavior and signaling will bring you in relationship with an entirely different, and more healthy, type of man."

Within a few weeks, she found that that was exactly what was happening. She practiced diligently imagining her parents were different, and she stopped seeing the two-timer she was involved with. She found herself being courted by three sound, solvent men, unlike any she had been attracted to before. The exercise she used is called "reimprinting."

Reimprinting

This technique reprograms your unconscious to seek out the kind of healthy, happy partner you would really want to be with. When you prepare to do this exercise, remember the following points. You do not have to be limited by your past. What you are doing is not forgetting or denying the past, simply showing your unconscious healthy, attractive, positive imagery that allows it to create an alternative pattern of attraction. The repetition of family patterns worked on you like hypnosis, and as a child you were unable to criticize them. The repetition of this exercise works in the same way. You don't need to comment on it or have faith in it. You just need to do it with energy and interest.

Remember: the unconscious responds to vividly imagined scenes in just the same way as it responds to real actions and memories. It does not judge truth or falsity. You don't have to believe that the scenes you imagine did or could have happened. You simply have to picture them over and over again. If your critical conscious mind complains they are unbelievable, don't worry. You don't need to believe them, you need to witness them. Having an alternative script for the past gives you an alternative script for the future.

1. Remember how your parents were when you were a child. Get out old pictures and remember vividly how things were.

2. Remember exactly how they treated each other, especially the bad times.

3. Now write down how they treated each other.

4. Then decide how you would like them to have behaved.

5. Decide also what sort of behavior and feelings you would like to have in your relationships in the present.

6. Now, using the pictures and sounds of how your parents were when you were a child, make up scenes of your parents getting on well with each other, expressing love for each other, working together, and being relaxed, happy and loving together.

7. Run these scenes over and over again in your mind until they are as familiar as your own face in the mirror.

Invisible hypnosis

Another client's case also showed me how powerful parental patterns and family hypnosis can be, and how we can be totally unaware for years of the influence they have over us. Jamie's relationship with Kate was on and off for seven years. It ended when he had an affair with Kate's best friend. Jamie was traumatized when Kate refused to see him again. In the past, Kate had always taken him back after his affairs. This time she would not and Jamie was heartbroken. He was also very confused. Why was he now heartbroken over Kate, when he had treated her so badly?

Jamie and I explored his feelings until we came to the beliefs that lay beneath them. Essentially he felt that his affair was a mistake and now he wanted Kate so much he wanted to marry her. I asked if he had wanted to marry her before and he said no. I asked him why not.

Jamie replied it was because he was so unfaithful. I pointed out that this was a circular argument. He could equally say he was unfaithful because he had decided not to marry her. I asked if there were any other reasons.

Jamie looked shocked and then ashamed. Then he told me that whenever he had an argument with Kate he told himself that it meant she wasn't the woman for him. Rationally he knew that it was ridiculous to imagine a couple could live together and never argue, but emotionally every argument to him meant the end.

I asked him to remember how his parents argued and made up. He thought for a long time and told me he could not remember his parents arguing. He told me that he had few memories of them together because his father was so often away on business. I asked if he ever had any arguments with his parents. Because his father was often away, the arguments he had were all with his mother and every one of them had followed the same frustrating pattern. She would refuse to listen to anything she disagreed with, so their arguments were never resolved.

Jamie had no model for resolving arguments in intimate relationships. His parents never argued in front of him, and his mother refused to engage when he argued with her. He had never witnessed his intimate-relationship role models have an argument, let alone resolve one. And his mother's refusal to listen when he argued with her meant that he had no experience of arguing to a satisfactory conclusion with a close family member.

He exclaimed, "That's why I always want things to be perfect! I'm trying to find a situation where there are no arguments." Romantically that meant he ended up having one affair after another because sooner or later he discovered some reason why the relationship was not perfect. As soon as he and his girlfriend had a disagreement he felt it was useless to persevere. Emotionally he felt helpless. Having no way to confront or deal with difficulty or accept it as a natural part of a relationship, he simply moved on. Instead of challenging the flaw of his own perfectionism, he carried on searching for the flawless partner. Jamie became absent in his relationships just as his father had been absent for his mother. But whereas in his parents' generation people tended to stay married, in Jamie's generation more and more people are divorcing or never marrying in the first place.

As he understood his patterns, Jamie realized how oblivious he had been. Then he laughed. "That's another thing I learned from my mother: how to ignore contradictions that are staring me in the face." Jamie's ability to explore his love for Kate had been blocked by the imprinting of his childhood. He also realized that wanting to marry Kate after the relationship had finished was just as extreme and idealistic as his belief that every argument spelt the end. One attitude was the mirror image of the other.

Jamie's case shows how being honest with our emotions will lead us to the core beliefs that are influencing us. But Jamie didn't just want insight, he wanted to change himself, so he practiced reimprinting every day for three weeks. He rang me sometime later to tell me that he was happily seeing a woman he would never have dreamed he could date a year ago.

6

How can I feel better about myself?

Who hasn't thought, I wish I felt better about myself? A few years ago I was having dinner with a group of New Age self-development trainers. They were full of wild and way-out ideas about how to improve the human condition. As the conversation got more and more animated, one of them said, "Wouldn't it be fantastic if there was some way we could just inject children with self-esteem so that they grew up really believing in themselves and able to fulfill their potential?"

"There is a way," I said. "It's called love." If we love our children we give them self-esteem.

Parents have to do two crucial emotional jobs for children: give them love and give them authority. Authority is teaching them "Do it this way, not that way. Be polite, be honest, take responsibility for your actions, look both ways before you cross the street . . ." and so on.

Love says, "You are a good idea. Whatever you do, we want you to be here." Love values a person just for existing, because they are alive and their life is beautiful and precious. Love is separate from authority. It doesn't love clever people more than slower ones. It doesn't stop loving just because someone didn't do what they were told. Love loves regardless, just as authority says regardless of how much you are loved you still have to learn how to behave properly with other members of society.

All parents want to give love and authority to their children but some express it more clearly than others. It is not necessary for parents to say any particular words to convey the message. The message is often more powerfully conveyed through ways of being and through actions than through words.

When you have received enough love, and felt the love you've been given, it teaches you that you yourself are valuable. Even when you get things wrong, or make mistakes, you are still as important and valuable as any other person on the planet. Whatever is going on outside, inside you know you are a good idea.

That is the key to happiness and robust self-esteem: Deep inside you know you are valuable, so when you need it, you can remember that just being you is always good enough. Unfortunately there are plenty of things, events and people nowadays who cause us to forget that, and lead us to seek our sense of value outside ourselves.

The consumer culture all around us offers an overwhelming number of ways to get instant self-esteem. Buy those shoes! That coat! That car! That house with the swimming pool! And it is not just the things—the clothes, the toys and the status symbols—it is the brands too.

Brands are emotional triggers. Vast sums of money are spent through advertising and in all sorts of other less-obvious ways to ensure that when you see a brand, or a crucial design element associated with it, particular emotions are triggered in you. Very often it is done so subtly and elegantly that you don't even notice it happening. But, let me assure you, it is still happening.

Many years ago I had a very telling personal experience of this. One Sunday evening I was shopping for groceries and I happened to be feeling fairly low and tired. I needed some beer. I didn't have that much money with me and I was dithering about what to buy. My indecision was probably caused by my tiredness and low spirits. I picked up a pack of the supermarket's own brand of lager, but then I wasn't quite sure I wanted it, so I put it back. Then I picked up a pack of well-known brand lager. I noticed that I suddenly felt distinctly better.

Years before this incident took place, the brand had run a big campaign of cinema advertisements that conveyed status, power and strength with imposing images of castles. I had remembered liking the advertisements, but I hadn't thought of them for years, and I didn't think of them at that time in the supermarket. It was simply that when I picked up that well-known brand of beer I felt better. The brand triggered the feeling.

I was fascinated. I put down the well-known one and picked up the store's own brand. I felt low and dissatisfied again. Rationally I knew that the beer inside the cans was almost identical, but holding the store's brand just didn't feel the same. I put down the store's brand and picked up the top brand. Magic! I felt better. So I bought the well-known brand. I didn't get the boost to my feelings from the beer, just from the brand. It was more expensive than the supermarket stuff, but the way I felt that day, feeling that much better was worth paying a little bit extra for.

Now that I know more about the internal mechanisms that sustain our self-esteem, I still feel it was a bargain. But I also know that if I feel low, and I don't want to spend an entire paycheck, it is much better to spend five minutes at home replenishing my energy and self-esteem for free, rather than using brands to do it for me. Brands do for self-esteem what smoking does for relaxation. They substitute an external source of good feeling for your natural internal one. In the long term, borrowing your good feelings from elsewhere prevents you developing your own inner re-sources. It is better to replenish your self-esteem from in-side than to borrow your good feelings from a brand.

Relationships are a zone in which we can be lured into borrowing self-esteem from our partner. In a healthy partnership it is no bad thing to give each other a boost, but rocky relationships can lower our self-esteem. If you turn to the partner you are having trouble with to boost your self-confidence you are not so likely to get what you need.

When your partner then walks out, it is a very painful blow. Who hasn't thought, "They left because there's something wrong with me"? Who wouldn't like to know that thought is nonsense?

Restoring and boosting your self-esteem is the next step on your path to health and happiness.

MAXWELL MALTZ

More than thirty years ago Dr. Maxwell Maltz, a plastic surgeon, wrote a bestselling book called *Psycho-Cybernetics* that revolutionized how we understand personalities. Dr. Maltz noticed that altering the physical appearance of his patients through surgery often created a remarkable change in personality. When people looked different they felt different. People who had been shy and lacking in confidence blossomed into confident outgoing types who enjoyed life to the full.

But what puzzled him was that some of his patients did not seem to get happier. Some, whose operations had changed their appearance from unusual to noticeably attractive, didn't seem to change their feelings at all. They still felt and behaved as though they had a reason to be depressed and unhappy with themselves.

Dr. Maltz concluded that cosmetic correction didn't benefit the patient if their inner image of themselves was poor. As he put it, they were "scarred on the inside." His solution was to create for those patients a visualization technique that changed their inner self-image. He had amazing results. When his patients changed the way they thought about themselves, they became happier and more fulfilled and their self-esteem rocketed. **Change yourself on the inside and the outside world changes too.** When I have taught people this technique they have told me their careers and social life have been transformed.

SELF-ESTEEM BOOSTER

The principle that Dr. Maltz used can be used by all of us who have had our self-esteem knocked by the end of a relationship. Here is how to restore your self-esteem by re-optimizing your self-image.

1. Imagine yourself as you would ideally like to be. Think about how you would look if you were as happy and confident as you wanted to be. How do you walk? What do you wear? What expressions are on your face? Where do you go? Take as much time as you need to see how you look when you are confident and full of self-esteem.

2. When you know what you will look like, make a little movie clip in your imagination of yourself, happy, confident and self-assured.

3. Now, imagine stepping into yourself in that movie. See what you see, hear what you hear and feel the confidence of being there and enjoying being exactly how you want to be.

4. Imagine waking up tomorrow as your ideal self feeling this good, and imagine the day going exactly as you want it to.

In order to get the maximum benefit from this technique, you must use it every day for at least a week. Carry on using later too, as often as you want. Each time it boosts your self-esteem—and it's fun too!

SELF-FULFILLING PROPHECIES

A self-image works like a self-fulfilling prophecy. We've all met people who are not classically good-looking and yet think of themselves as attractive and as a result have an aura about them. Equally there are plenty of people who think of themselves as unattractive, who unconsciously sabotage any attempts to appear attractive. Anyone who truly believes they are unattractive won't represent themselves at their best and people will inevitably find them unattractive. In a similar vein, studies have shown that people who earn more than they believe they are worth feel uncomfortable with the extra amount. So they spend it, or lend it, or find some other way to get rid of it.

It is possible to have a strong, positive self-image in one area of life, for example in business, and a weak self-image in another, say public speaking. Our self-image is a very powerful influence. We don't necessarily get what we want in life, but we generally get what we expect. We all live up to or down to our expectations. Quite simply, you can never be better on the outside than you believe yourself to be on the inside.

How you think of yourself also affects how other people feel about you because they are constantly responding to your body language, the tone of your voice and the emotional signals you are transmitting. All day long people are interpreting the congruency between your verbal communication and the non-verbal signals of the emotions that lie behind it. If your self-esteem is low you might be saying confident words but showing unconfident body language. By improving your inner self-image you can have all the confidence you want. You can not only like and trust yourself more, but be liked and trusted more by others as well. Your possibilities at any moment in life are computed from your self-image, your psychological blueprint.

Imagine I walk down the street and I see my ex chatting and laughing with another person. They are clearly enjoying each other's company. I have an automatic response in my abdomen. I feel shocked and winded. What is my next response? Do I experience negative thoughts and feelings of loss, fear, anger and jealousy? Do I pretend to ignore the feeling? Or do I feel free to wish them well and go about my business? My automatic response will be determined by my self-image.

If I feel negative, sad, angry or lonely when I see my ex, I need to improve my self-image. I may be tempted to try to get my ex to talk to me, or ask them to do something to make me feel better, but ultimately this cannot work. No other person can reach inside us and change our feelings for us. If I really want to feel better, it is not my ex who needs to change, but me. I need to change my self-image. If I see myself as successful, kind and confident, I can experience the shock of seeing my ex in this different context without being drawn into negative feelings about him or her. I keep my cool because internally I feel good about myself.

In situations like this I don't have time to think and then choose my reaction. I react automatically according to my inner sense of myself. My self-image is my inner sense of myself, to which I refer unconsciously all the time to see how to behave or perform. In other words, my reactions are founded in my self-image. Building a positive self-image ensures that your automatic reactions come from a sense of freedom, confidence and empowerment.

INTERNAL DIALOGUE

For many people our internal imagery is the most influential part of our thinking. For others, what we say to ourselves and how we say it has a greater effect on our feelings than the pictures we make. Consider, for example, your internal dialogue. Your internal dialogue is the inner voice you use to think with. We often use it when we are making decisions or working things out. We use the internal dialogue when we are worried or criticizing ourselves.

Think now of the last time you used that inner voice to comment on your relationship. Remember what you were saying to yourself, remember the particular sentence you used, or a typical thing you would have said to yourself. Repeat the comment to yourself but change the tone of the voice. Keep saying exactly the same words, but make the tone of the voice different. Make it happy or excited. Make it friendly or funny. Make it sound like a cartoon character. Try out all sorts of different tones of voice with exactly the same words until you find a tone that makes you feel completely different and better.

Now choose a different voice. Choose an encouraging voice, the voice of a friend or a film star, or a voice with an accent you really like. You can play with your inner voice in many more ways. You can speed it up or slow it down. You can make it higher or lower. Keep changing it until you have found the characteristics that make it friendly and supportive.

Whenever you find yourself using your inner voice to talk about your situation, use this new voice to make yourself feel better. You can still hear exactly the same words and learn from whatever you are thinking but there is no need to feel bad unnecessarily.

If you want to make even more changes you can. Say a bit more to yourself. Now notice where you made that voice. Does it sound as if it is right in the middle of your head or towards the front? Is it to one side of your head or at the back, or is it outside? Wherever it is, imagine it moving. Move it left a bit, right a bit, up a bit and down a bit. Now move it down to the bottom of your neck and from there along to the top of your shoulder. Imagine how it would sound from there. Next move it down to your elbow and finally to the tip of your thumb. What does it feel like hearing the voice from there? Keep experimenting until you find the place to put it where it feels most comfortable to listen to.

Now that you've changed how you hear it, listen once more to what you were saying. Do you feel better? Do you feel as good as you would like? If not, there is something more to do. Now that you hear your inner voice like this maybe you would like to reconsider the words you have been using. Do you swear at yourself?

Do you say something like "You stupid idiot, you really screwed up this time," or "How could I be so dumb?"

Nearly all of us use vicious language to beat ourselves up when we think we've made a mistake. That is not very helpful, as the purpose of self-criticism is to improve our performance and stop us repeating our mistakes. The inner dialogue has a positive intent, but frequently uses punitive expressions. But if you think about it, you wouldn't want anyone else to talk to you like that, so there is no need to put up with it from yourself. It might be a bit much to say, "Oh good, another learning experience!" but you can definitely make some positive changes. Experiment with less aggressive language. Ask yourself, "What is the positive intention behind this bad language?"

The best form of criticism is constructive, so see if you can find something to say that specifically points the way to making things better. A good way to find a better form of words is to ask yourself how you would talk to a younger person whom you were helping to deal with a problem. So, instead of cursing or nagging yourself, try using kinder, more encouraging words to guide yourself towards what you want.

Somebody Who Loves You

There are many, many ways to feel better and boost your self-esteem. Here are some more of them. When we are feeling low, it is a commonplace that our friends and family can see our strengths and values when we ourselves do not. We can use this to access our self-esteem if for any reason we have become depressed or self-doubting.

1. Close your eyes and think of someone who loves or deeply appreciates you. Remember how they look and imagine they are standing in front of you.

2. Now imagine stepping out of your body and into the body of the person who loves you. See through their eyes, hear through their ears and feel their love and good feelings as they look at you.

3. Notice in detail what it is that they love and appreciate about you. Fully understand these amazing qualities that perhaps you hadn't appreciated about yourself until now. Take a few moments to feel good as you look at yourself.

4. Notice where the feeling is strongest and give it a color.

5. Imagine spreading that color all through you, up to the top of your head and down to the tips of your toes.

6. Now double its intensity and brightness.

7. As you open your eyes keep that feeling glowing inside you. You can keep that inner feeling with you for hours and hours and rerun this exercise whenever you want to boost it. The more you do it, the easier it becomes, and eventually it becomes automatic to love and feel loved. It is a great habit to have.

Confidence is hardwired

Occasionally people tell me that they are worried the self-esteem they are creating might not last. They are worried that it is fake, or it doesn't belong to them. There are two important things I tell them to reassure them, and I'm going to share them with you too.

Firstly, everyone has a right to self-esteem. It is a natural gift to us from our parents. Not all parents are as good at giving it to us as we or they might wish, but ultimately it is what every parent would give a child if they were free to do so.

Secondly, and even more importantly, self-confidence, the core of self-esteem, is innate. It is built into us from birth. Some of us lose touch with it and learn to worry or distrust ourselves. Worry and distrust are learned, and can be unlearned. But the confidence is hardwired. It is there all the time underneath our worries.

You can see a demonstration of the universal, built-in nature of self-confidence whenever you see a baby learning to walk. Babies learn to walk before they can talk and before they understand the words being said to them. When they are learning to walk they tumble and fall to the floor over and over again. But they pick themselves up and try again. They fall over hundreds of times, and they keep on trying. They keep going because the confidence they have isn't learned, it isn't created by other people's encouragement, it is innate. They simply trust that sooner or later they will succeed. They have a fundamental, instinctive confidence that their persistence will be rewarded. And as a result, it is.

That confidence is hardwired into all of us. We all still have it. Everything in this chapter is just a way of reminding you of what you already have.

THE FRIENDLY MIRROR

My friend Michael Breen devised an excellent technique that I love to show people because it instantly makes you feel good about how you look. You can do this any time you are in a room with a mirror. Many people condition themselves to feel bad by looking in the mirror and thinking about wrinkles or fat. This technique turns that on its head and conditions you to feel happy about your appearance.

1. Sit yourself down where you can turn to look at a mirror, but don't look at it just yet.

2. Think of a time when someone you know to be sincere paid you a compliment.

3. Remember what they said, and hear it again in your mind and remember how it made you feel.

4. Imagine that feeling of being complimented, loved and cherished spreading through you like ink spreading through blotting paper, the more it spreads the more powerful it gets.

5. Now turn and look at yourself in the mirror.

6. Enjoy it!

7. Finally, imagine taking a picture of yourself just like that. Imagine taking that picture right into your heart. Keep it there so that you can look at it whenever you want to remind yourself how good you can feel.

7

FALLING IN LOVE AGAIN

Have you heard the saying "Love conquers all"? It is an excellent illustration of the dangers of trying to sum up relationships in a neat, memorable phrase. It sounds like such a wonderful, noble sentiment. But "Love conquers all" is ambiguous; it can mean two quite different things.

It can mean "True love is a force which will make everything work out, whatever I do." Or it can mean, "True lovers are so committed to each other that they will rise to any challenge and overcome any obstacle to make sure each other is safe and happy and that they can be together."

There is a world of difference between the two. The first one means "Because I love, love will do all the hard work for me," and the second means, "Because I love, I will do all the hard work."

NO MAGIC FORMULA

A lot of the work of a relationship is facing and resolving conflicts. I don't know a formula for a conflict-free relationship. In fact, it seems that conflict is an essential part of life. But every now and then we all ask, Does it have to be so difficult? After all, as maverick therapist Frank Farrelly says, "Men and women both want the same things: sex, love and security. They just want them in a different order."

We all dream of the perfect relationship—the perfect kiss, the ultimate passion, the total understanding—we all know what "love" is. We all know what to do when we feel it. But how do we know? Where do these ideas come from?

IDEAS OF LOVE

The traditions of love evolved gradually over many, many centuries. For most of our history life was very, very different from how it is now. It was tougher, shorter, more dangerous. All our traditions about the passions and perils of love, about fidelity and fickleness, about sexuality and commitment, come from a world in which making love had serious consequences.

When making love was likely to get you pregnant,

people generally didn't do it lightly. The chances were that if you slept with someone regularly, you could be landed with them for life. So people took far longer to choose whom to sleep with. And relationships were not just about love. A marriage was an important economic arrangement. Life was hard and labor-intensive and each sex had a clear role to play. Children were not an optional extra; they were an investment. They were expected to look after you in your old age.

All societies developed courtship rituals to channel and control natural sex drives. Courtship was a formalized way of flirting. At the same time, perhaps because the sex drive had to be sublimated, they created ideals, myths and fantasies that were so popular and alluring they survived long after the courtship rituals disappeared.

RECENT CHANGES

Throughout the last two centuries the situation changed more and more. Science and technology had a huge impact on our health, culture and environment. Then in the 1960s came the pill. The invention of simple, cheap, reliable contraception changed courtship patterns forever. Now we are able to make love without the risk of pregnancy. So more of us do so, more often, with more people. We now have freedoms undreamed of by our grandparents' generation. Yet we have inherited from them, and the generations before them, all the desires, beliefs and fantasies that come from the age of courtship.

The ideal of having a monogamous partnership and

children is so deeply rooted in our culture that it has an enormous influence on us. As a result, the commonest aspiration of men and women is to find a partner, fall in love and settle down together. But what we want and what we do don't necessarily match up anymore.

A recent survey has found that the average length of a relationship in which the partners live together, including marriages, has shrunk to seven years. At the time of writing, a quarter of all children in the United Kingdom are brought up by single parents and more people are single and living on their own than ever before. There is little social or economic pressure to get married now, but there is pressure to be a successful, financially productive individual. Nowadays we see less of our extended families and do less socializing outside the home than previous generations. That forces partners to provide far more for each other than ever before in terms of recreation and psychological and emotional support.

In some ways relationships are easier; in other ways, harder. Society no longer makes us conform to specific, rigid roles. But equally it no longer supports any particular roles either. You can no longer expect a partner of either sex to fit in to an established role. If you want a relationship to last nowadays, you have to maintain it yourself.

Whatever your family did, whatever your cultural background, ultimately your destiny and your relationships are up to you.

Being successful

When you feel better you will naturally find that the possibility of another relationship arises. Since the last one hurt this can be scary, even though you have changed so much. But now you have plenty of reasons to feel stronger. Strangely enough, when I finish working with a client, there is nearly always one more issue to be sorted out, one they never expect. I call it the challenge of success. In other words, taking fully on board the fact that you really have achieved the change you desired. So many of us have learned little ways of putting ourselves down or accepting second best that it takes a while to realize that you can be successful. You are now a better, happier person than you used to think. That's why I ask people to repeat the techniques in chapter 6 many times to embed thoroughly the new sense of success and positive self-image in your mind and body.

Getting used to being successful means changing your expectations about forming new relationships. The ideas in this chapter have all come from talking to clients about how they adjust to success. I am not claiming to be the world's greatest expert. I am just sharing some ideas that have been gathered from people who have gone this way before. Each of us has a slightly different journey, but some of my clients have told me how helpful they found it to write down some of the thoughts and ideas that were useful to them. Here I have written down the things that I and my clients have found useful, so that if you want to you can use them too.

Reaching success teaches us to be more curious and welcoming to new experiences, and the idea of trying something new changes from frightening to attractive. When you know you can be successful you don't need to hurry. You can enjoy the journey. Meeting people and seeing them and flirting all become a pleasure in themselves. You don't have to worry about the outcome. When you are not in a hurry, you can enjoy things for what they are. And now you can decide what sort of relationship you want. You don't have to fit into anyone else's expectations if you don't want to. By the same token, if you want a traditional relationship, you don't have to pretend otherwise or be ashamed of it. A lot of other people want one too. And if you are looking for a serious relationship you don't have to go to any particular place; the right meeting can happen anywhere.

It is a good idea to treat all men and women with equal kindness and politeness, but it is not so good to bend what you think in order to accommodate others. There is no need to twist yourself up to please other people. You can ask yourself instead, "What pleases me?" Your likes and dislikes are as valid as anyone else's.

If you make yourself comfortable, then the people you talk to will feel more at ease with you. That's why, when you meet someone of the opposite sex, instead of saying to yourself, "Will they like me?," it is easier to ask yourself, "How will this person make me happy?" It makes everyone feel more comfortable when you assume you are always good enough and that other people find you attractive. It also frees you to think, "Who do I want to talk to?"

You are interesting if you are interested. The essence

of flirting is enjoying the presence of the other person. It is not trying it on; it is not trying too hard. Most people feel good if they make someone else happy. When you let someone know they are doing that for you, it is a powerful invitation to them to continue.

The more you understand yourself, the more you will understand other people, because fundamentally we are all the same. The less you pretend and the less you put yourself down, the easier it is to spot other people who are doing it. The more honest you are to yourself, the more you will find yourself attracted, and attractive, to other people who are honest.

You will also find that you give up using negative phrases when you talk to yourself. The unconscious mind does not have a negative mode. For example, if I say to you, "Don't think of elephants," what happens? You think, however briefly, of elephants, and then try to say "no" to the thought. If you dwell on what you don't want, you are more likely to get what you don't want. An important psychological law is that **you are more likely to get whatever you focus on.** So, being successful, you will naturally want to create a habit of speaking positively and thinking of what you *do* want.

Then, when you do that, go for it. If you dream of going out with someone, do something about it. If the answer is no, you'll save yourself time. If the answer is yes, enjoy it. If you are frightened of making a fool of yourself, remember that being willing to risk making a fool of yourself is a brave act. Your courage might be just the thing that convinces them you are worth getting to know better.

Finally, go slowly. You already know that you can start a relationship, but see what happens if you go a little slower than usual. Some people are really keen to have a partner or to get to the stage of having sex. Others rush just as keenly towards markers of commitment such as meeting the family, moving in and so on. This time, take it a bit more slowly. Enjoy the moment that Pooh Bear thought was the best moment of all—the moment just before you eat the honey.

CHOOSING A NEW RELATIONSHIP

In these last two sections, I've collected a few ideas that might be useful as you meet people and maybe start dating, or start a new relationship. These are not rules, they are just ideas that I, and some of the people I have worked with over the years, have found useful. One way or another, most of us know a lot of this already, but we have forgotten it, or forget to use it when we need it. I have put it all into bullet form here so that it is easy to dip into when you want to remind yourself. Use them as much, or as little, as you want.

• **Keep your options open** for a while. Don't be discouraging or cheat, or lie, but don't let a potential partner assume you two have become a couple just because you like each other and have gone out a couple of times. It is instructive to see how people behave when they feel there is a bit of competition, or uncertainty. What's more, it is useful to see other people to make comparisons. Anyone can be fascinating if you really concentrate on them, but don't let mere fascination tip you into a relationship.

• **Take time before you judge** a possible partner. Don't trust them straightaway either. Find out a bit more. If you take your time you'll learn whether you are reacting to your own expectations or unconscious projections. This time round you will probably discover that some things you used to think important don't matter so much. It is intriguing to find out how your tastes change.

• **It is OK to be embarrassed** occasionally. We all have our little vanities and vulnerabilities. In fact, as we saw, vulnerability is valuable. When you are dating someone, you may impress them with your wit and charm and looks, but you get closer when your vulnerability and ineptitude show as well.

• **Welcome the unexpected.** It is how we cope with things when they don't go according to plan that reveals our true colors. However glamorous your exterior, it is the inner, vulnerable, imperfect self who is capable of intimacy. A good predictor of a successful relationship is not whether the partners love each other's best points, but how well they deal with each other's weaknesses and foolishness.

• **There is no hurry.** The price of love is taking the risk of being hurt, as you have already found out. Before you get in too deep, decide whether you are willing to pay. If not, go back to stage one until you are ready. You are ready for a relationship when you are willing to take that risk, not when you think you need a relationship because you feel lonely, poor or left out.

- **Meet their friends.** They will tell you, or show you, quite a bit about this person. And a long-term relationship is not just an affair between two people; it is a meeting of two tribes. They don't all have to get on, but you will have to find a way to fit in or duck out of relationships with your partner's friends. If your partner does not make an effort to introduce you to their friends, find out why. It is not a good sign for long-term stability to be kept apart from the rest of your partner's life.

- **Find your match.** A partner who provides some opposition can be good for you. You do not want a doormat, unless all you want to do for the rest of your life is wipe your feet. If you want someone to bring out the best in you, choose someone who can stand up to you. We fight people in order to find out if they are strong enough to trust with our defense. A doormat is not a very good line of defense.

- **Use an external point of view.** If you are not sure whether you ought to do something or not, imagine that someone you love and respect happened to come across you doing it. If you would be proud of yourself, that's fine. If you would be embarrassed, that's fine—but if you would you be ashamed to be seen doing it, don't do it.

- Above all, **set your standards high.** Don't make excuses for people, don't lower your standards and don't stoop to anyone. Get any suitor to rise up to you. A relationship should bring out the best in you and your partner, so it is not worth settling for second best from anyone.

STARTING A NEW RELATIONSHIP

• **There is no perfect attitude for relationships.** Sometimes we need to be strong, and sometimes gentle. The key is to be free from fixed patterns so that you can respond to the moment. However much you feel you've learned from your recent experiences, try not to lecture your partner. Just do what you respect in yourself and ask for what you want.

• **Be honest** at the beginning of a relationship. Honesty can be painful, but it is less painful in the end than lying. Equally, don't try to be totally honest about everything all at once. It is too overwhelming for most of us to have a whole life story at one sitting. It is also too easy to get carried away and exaggerate things. Take your time and listen as well.

• **Be honest, but be discreet.** The focus of your life and your attention should be on the present and the future. No new partner should want to hear every last detail of your past relationships. If you find that you feel you want to talk about the past in great detail, it is probably an indication that you still have some emotional issues you have not yet dealt with. Your past is your job to deal with. It is not your new partner's job. So, rather than foist it on them, work through it with a friend or a therapist.

• **Make an extra effort.** At the beginning of a relationship, in-love-ness is like a fabulous glow that makes the ordinary delightful and the difficult easy. The first time round we think life will be like this forever. We find out it won't. Sooner or later we realize that it is a gift that can be used. While you are protected and encouraged by in-love-ness, lay the foundation for loving.

• **If you disagree with your partner, appreciate the difference.** Your partner's different point of view should be an asset to you, not a hindrance. It lets you see life from two angles. At the same time, it doesn't help to ignore your own wishes. If you go along with things you don't like, your partner will assume you don't mind. If you do mind, tell them.

• **A relationship is what you do together.** It is not what you dream about doing, or think about doing, or talk about doing: It is what you do. If all you do is talk, then that is your relationship.

• When you begin to think of yourself as part of a couple, it is another chance to become conscious of your own unconscious behavior. Watch the old family imprinting come up, and this time be aware of your new alternatives. **This time round you don't have to fly on autopilot.** You can pick and choose.

• **Remember that manipulation is inevitable.** It is part of the games people play, so be good-humored about it. It arises very often from defensiveness or sheer habit. If you spot your partner trying to manipulate you, notice it and acknowledge it but don't condemn them. We've all had years of training in being manipulative and indirect, and it takes a saint, and a humorless one at that, to be perfectly straight all the time. Be prepared to laugh more often. Try to ensure that your partner can share the joke.

• **Laugh at yourself.** You are brave, beautiful and ridiculous, just like the rest of us. If you laugh at yourself, you give your partner permission to laugh at you too. And tease your partner. Teasing should be fun. It is not the same as picking on someone, or rubbing salt in their wounds, or being sarcastic. Teasing is affectionate, and it targets our vanities not our vulnerabilities.

• **This time round, say or do something you found really difficult** in your last relationship. Each relationship is a chance to step further along in your personal evolution. Deep down you are looking for someone to share that journey with you. A new relationship is a chance to go further towards self-knowledge and further towards love than you have been before. Don't let your old habits move back in to inhibit you or limit you. Go further than you went last time. For some of us, it was difficult to ask for help or to be seen to be weak. If that was you, ask for help, just once, and see what happens. Other people find it difficult to bring thoughtfulness to their passion. They throw themselves at a partner and abandon all restraint. Well, if that was you, just this once, go a little slower, put the brakes on your runaway feelings, let your partner's feelings take the lead and see what happens. Stretch yourself. If a relationship is really going to work, it will change you by taking you further towards your own truth. We all have a lot of habits, beliefs and behaviors to shed. A good relationship will help you do that.

• **Don't expect to win every argument.** Arguing is necessary and healthy, but it must lead somewhere. If you are arguing, stick to the subject. If you both find that difficult, write down what you are disagreeing about and stick to that point until you have reached an agreement. Then stop. Don't drag up the past or throw in personal insults, and don't try to guilt-trip your partner. Be prepared to win or lose an argument gracefully.

• **Value yourself.** When you value yourself you treat yourself and your wishes with respect. We can be loving and generous and happy, but it is important to recognize that we all have selfish wants. If we don't ask for what we want consciously, our desire tends to come out in unconscious, uncontrolled and often unpleasant ways. If you don't ask, how will anyone know that you want it? If you don't get what you want, how will you know whether you really wanted it? If you don't stand up for your wants, they will haunt you. If you don't put your wants on the table, you can't bargain with your partner to reach a deal you are both happy with. If you do say what you want, you give permission to your partner to say what they want. Then the two of you can negotiate until you reach a situation where you are both pleased.

• **Remember love is an action.** In-love-ness is a gift from nature. Love is a gift from humans. To love someone, sooner or later you have to do something. So do it.

Finally, please use whatever works for you. This is just good stuff I've picked up over the years. If it helps you to find the truth in your relationship, it has more than done its job. Please don't just read it, and don't just take my word for it. Try it. Put it to the test. Test every single part of this with your own experience and find what works for you and what feeds your soul. Use anything and everything from here that helps you to build your life's success.

All the techniques throughout the book are available for you whenever you need them. And you will know when you don't need them anymore. You will feel happy, relaxed and confident and you'll be on your way to the richest most fulfilling relationship you've ever had. Enjoy it.

This is the last chapter from me. The next chapter is yours.

If you wish to train with

Paul McKenna personally,

call 011-44-845-230-2022

or visit

www.paulmckenna.com

Index of techniques

ALSO BY
PAUL MCKENNA

CHANGE YOUR LIFE IN 7 DAYS
1-4000-8287-0 • $23.00 hardcover

With his clear and clever program, the world's leading hypnotist shows how to control your mind, change your outlook, and vastly improve your life in one week.

Wherever books are sold
CrownPublishing.com